Arcadia Road

A TRILOGY

Also by Thorpe Moeckel

Poetry

Meltlines (chapbook)

Odd Botany

Making a Map of the River

Venison

Off Owl's Head (e-chapbook)

Nonfiction

*Watershed Days: Adventures
(a Little Thorny & Familiar) in the Home Range*

Arcadia Road

A TRILOGY

THORPE MOECKEL

etruscan press

Etruscan Press
Wilkes University
84 West South Street
Wilkes-Barre, PA 18766
(570) 408-4546

www.etruscanpress.org

Published 2015 by Etruscan Press
Printed in the United States of America
Cover design by Michael Ress
Interior design and typesetting by Julianne Popovec
The text of this book is set in Electra.

First Edition

15 16 17 18 19 5 4 3 2 1

Library of Congress Cataloging-in-Publication Data

Moeckel, Thorpe.
 [Poems. Selections]
 Arcadia road : a trilogy / Thorpe Moeckel.
    pages ; cm
 ISBN 978-0-9897532-5-8
 I. Title.
 PS3613.O334A6 2015
 811'.6—dc23
                        2015005012

Please turn to the back of this book for a list of the sustaining funders of Etruscan Press.

To William and Ola

Arcadia Road

A TRILOGY

Arcadia Road

A TRILOGY

VENISON

I start with an incision behind the tendon,
but before that I've gutted the buck, covered

his eyes with leaves, walked around dizzy,
watching how he fell, how he ran to fall, bullet

having taken a dam out, dam that holds a life
together, place in air where air has known

more than air, if flesh & cells aren't air
of sorts, the way a person who says he loves

may love the idea of loving that person or just
the idea of who that person could become given

the stuff, enough of what we mean but don't say
when we say love; & I've studied the bloodtrail

in the leaves, departure's skidmarks to say it
rudely considering there may be only arrival,

more arrival like continually to the moment
and moment before I pulled the trigger – unsafetied

bound – all moment & arrival in the arriving
precision in the gash some few are stumbling, looking

for the punchlines of, the line with the punch & punch
with the line, that movement of finger as told by eye

and less & more even than some leaf or squirrel
or barkflake trunkwards, lichen, scat of bobcat, hawk,

all sirens, triggers & triggered too – the knife is
still sharp as the line the bullet sliced, worm of it, &

I've read the red path that marks the last living,
the shock & sting & shock of the sting I shot

forward to – spinning, rifled – to grillsizzle, loin,
full table, friends, or earlier the fragrance, humid

as kissing, essence of bone & scrap in the crockpot
overnight on low then slopped among the slop

and pails, gates & latches, to the dog bowls, a bit
for the barn cats. To dwell is to spin, orbit & spin forth

and in, & in through no out till breath do us heart
and track & pattern. The wood, sycamore branch

knobby & bootbusted, hangs by fist of braided poly
through rafter in an isosceles, & you could talk family here,

knots & ties, but the other end's loose until by grunt
and heave, slip & shimmie, the deer hangs in the shed

as some deer must do, the ones it has been said come
to us, know our scents as we cannot know how

such nose knowledge geographizes the scape
even standing among oak & hazel, sky a pearl

in the unmaking, stiff wind blending leafcrunch
and limbscreech with the blossoming that between

the shadows is a space equal to trees & limbs,
the way that space & the light & the space between

the trees are, too, imperfect accuracies where sanctity
roots the winter through mulchdrunk to frostline

and grain belt of microflora, little feasties, mineralfest,
map of leafvein revealing the yearnings behind

growth, structure; no, I don't believe he came to me
whose legs wear the branch, a fastening to be unfastened

for future fastenings – knives, forks, marinades, mouths;
I believe it is less than that – the world does not reward

our imaginings that are our own rewards; the indifference,
nature if you will, cares a kind that's beyond us, that's

our reward, the darkness, unknowing even the hunger
to know anyway, not stubbornness so much as grip,

the cling of days, life's steel toes. So the deer hangs,
big ears splayed, antenna of antler worn vagrant ivory

beyond the last tine, blood at crux where as in scarlet
elbow socks I gripped in gutting time, & the plumbing –

intestine, liver, lung, so on – stirred a wiregrass
of yearning in vulture & fox; it hangs, some rootgrasp

in divinity's rhizomatica, & it isn't all becoming the blaze
of brindle, pale flank, pale chin, dark between

the legs that knew leap & hop a grace made more by
who can say? – say hunger, sheath; more even

than gracelessness, a kind of rain that won't start
or stop or differentiate from mist though the roof

is ice & the gravel is wet and the hogs are knocking
on feeder lid & I'm ripping skin, finger in membrane

along the upper inner thigh, starting a tear the tip
of the knife enters as a helicopter the airspace

above the garden when you're braiding baling twine
between bamboo stakes in April for the peas, chopping

its jet-fueled blades, calling attention to the peace
that now you've lost it you know you had, the way

in bed when the smoochies reach a saturation
you cannot let hope or its caffeinated pals skitch

you too radly across the frozen streets or else
the tendon, sliced, disallows a simple mortis & tenon

situation, and the deer no longer hangs with the relative
frictive ease of rigging, one knee required to keep it

from spinning as the knife leads to the dressing room
opening less as we tear certain envelopes as

what's in them tears us; thus I grip, yank, exposing
this astonishment of burgundy, all sinew & gleam,

pull some more, one flank then other, two strange
and radiant peninsulas that join at widest acreage

where the pelvis – not really a mainland – whispers
elementals so nimble they seem new each time in this

too dusty shed the ritual, as rituals must, turn now
to then & then to always, always this awake,

this motion & joinery among stacks of lumber,
spare sheetrock, junked enamel sinks, for

the soul of a shed is a place in cedars where
the leaves stay wet even after the sun enters

the doodle for a day after a day of rain, a place
where the deer moved in a too sightlessness

to do anything but listen to its steps. Once
from the middle of a river in a canoe I heard

a barking approach when from the left bank
a doe splashed into the shoals, the dogs close,

though it stayed ahead wearily until no flailing
final gesture but a laying down for the current

to have its implacable way, dogs turning back,
few last barks, & I casted for smallmouth, doe

drifting but not for long as now not longer
in the unpeeling the deer coatless might be

some mutant greyhound great dane mutt. How
live this way when the world makes it easy,

killingly, to drop by the mini mart, swipe plastic
and off you go with a made to order ham & cheese

on so called whole grain cloaked in foil it took
more energy to make & ship than the meat

will give; how come to know the woods
such that you dream them through the eyes of

the deer that you dream other nights is staring
at you, not the one you shot last week but one

that will cross some path with you soon as never
and may take a bullet or miss or greedy eyes on

it unaware ratcheting body aquiver, knees weak,
shaky until slower breathing like a small flame

in the corner of the stove – a deer like that to see
woods through the eyes of is a vision of what lives

in the nose, inhale not enough syllables for time
it takes to do it, not enough adjectives in quiver,

but such is sensation, some chimney sweep
ramming its brush down the pipe; how sit hours

in frozen woods looking at shapes, the everything in
nothing, past squirrels & shadows, for one deer

when you could be making a name for yourself,
selling something to someone who may need it

or want it, I don't know, maybe at home with wife
and kids, fixing the everything that always needs,

breaking other things breaking & fixing in flux,
sweet marrow, proximity of bodies known over time

and place, changes, awarenesses shifting, each day
if you're lucky – & you're lucky – the thing you'd

never notice or have been so long at forgot. I love
all tools but a loaded gun is a baby in my arms

on a cold morning cutting teeth and they slow,
not at all, only the weight, wood & steel, long heft

that becomes the becoming more part of you than
your arms as you hold the weapon and see

through what it holds and how that lethal load
is held & will reach, if sent, to your eyes that are

inseparable now from your arms, though ear & nose
have entered, powder & spark. Shoot, my hands hurt

real fine with the chill of a dead thing hanging days
in a shed and the underflesh holding cold as wood

tenants heat, generous too with my fingertips
as I work skin from membrane, a delicate butchery

though butchery cannot be delicate. Lower back,
lower ribs, and further down: neck, forelegs, sun

splintering through the rough cut boards, the jackass
Charlie looking at the deliberations through flecks

of the fence, ducks in winter-dead nettles, drilling
when necessary; rabbits in the hutch, their alfalfa,

waterers, horizons of wire, gridded, square on square,
not so different from our needs, hurts, losses –

molestations, you know the why & how & yearning –
structures, patterns: feeding, mating, earning, the way

the buck rubs in a line the cedar, the hazel sapling,
and beyond that, way out, in, its left tine on my shin

as the fleshlessness tries to spin on the rope while press
and steady debate their merits, hacksaw chewing through

neck bone, foreleg, hoofs coming off for stock, skin
on the fence, some phantom laundry. I wonder

what little stories wait beneath all flesh, that may
be told now through curves & shadows, clothes, only

a part, most essential & gratifying part, all that is
beautiful & right & on the surface but of the surface

more, as though the depth was all we had east or
west over, through, across; & a gun's anyway kin

to the leg of one you've loved long & not always
well & therefore softer, harder, that leg in your hands

and how you hold it every time the regard because
it's holding you as the beloved must brace us

in the reciprocities, flesh with which you've tremored,
let your best trees fall, no more windbreak, habitats

one place where it is night's turn to neglect fetching
the chocolate & the rivers are running clear because

they're dropping. The hardest part is over, the part
where things seen inside out become out inside

seen things where part the parts you've unhoused,
and there they are, mute inhabitants, ready to work

with you, grateful it seems, as if free, so lovely
the bondages behind believing in freedom; talking

quarters, loins, walls disassembled, rich cuts,
umbilicus of hip & belly, humidity's ward,

a few hairs to be plucked; and ligaments, swells,
rips, jetty & strand, a tube ride here with

left hand on sternum, right wearing the knife's
cherry handle the way longjohns stretch

on torso, scrub & grope & hump it, sponging
motion while trying on the scents: here

the blade, edge slow honed at the sink before
loading the stove one last time with oak this

sinew likely knows the acorns of, there being rub
last fall on adjacent cedar, but the smell is more

than oaky acorn tannin: cave passage, steel bucket,
moss as it's scraped from stone by fallen branch,

branching in – all branches in, tributaries to not,
that reprehensible flower past midnight blooming,

petalled variously as any adverb or shard, & veined,
ovulacious. Always that blue sheen on membrane

to bud my ridgiest canopy, fat billowy nimbus
between far & few; and the bottom weight

of severed shoulder, leap, swing, hand on shin,
plop it in cooler in further delamination – meat

is arithmeticked as breath, as nakedly dressed –
where to cut, pressure, angle, rhyme; the body

tells you body that is & not your own fissioning
sleekness lessening, expanding, the way you can tell

the weather by the woodsmoke after it leaves
the stovepipe – sometimes it slides the north pitch

and surfs the downdraft into gravel & the dogs barking,
cilantro in the coldframe: this means freezing rain

tomorrow noon, and the deer, another herd moving
hard tonight in expectation of say there's paw paw

downdrainage no critter's got to the fruit of, fallen
or not, & the sweet bounty is in the air. My job here

is simple – to feed the family, take apart, put together:
later these shoulders cleaned of membrane on the table –

Kirsten, Sophie, & I in a perforato of bladework,
trimming, carving – will be freezered in portions fit

for three, larger bags for company, gifts, trade; smell
of Sharpie labeling date & cut – dwelling, we were

in the dream of deer moving in the Geminid shower
through geographies of scent, paths in stickweed,

ravining, crossing the CSX, hoof on gravel, rail,
fox musk in the sinus, crows moonward where

spilt the sun's yolk on shoals, a few geese, otter
in boxelder's skirt, dozing; here are acorns – who

doesn't love acorns, napsize, frizz of cap, bell of them,
the way their red & yellows & browns ray ashimmer,

polished longitudinally on the unroundlessness.
I am standing in the shed. The deer is not a wind chime.

You know I am cutting after the nature of nature;
it is not knowledge but desire for the touch

that constitutes, a bringing into the body, a digestion,
less than sensory, cellular, less even than marrow

or politics of marrow, less at last than prayer. I feel
emptied doing this, as in a place & time where close

doesn't apply. The breath of God feels accurate, not
swimming but being a particle among the particular,

sediment in time's flood, the galactic pulse & trickle.
I am not feeding the family, the family is feeding me.

These are the sounds the knife makes, I hope,
and the heat of the skillet. The skillet. Such is travel.

There's love being made. There's no more bleeding.
The blood is in the ground. The sweeter the dead,

as they say, the sweeter the water. Do not look
at the eyes, look at what the knife sees along the spine,

twizzling the loin's long ridge from its bedrock
of bone, for what it sees is dead & not dead – there

are lives in each thread of the long, firm muscle
that knows no other motion as it hangs like some

trapper's bounty, gravity its only skeleton, heat
having left & with it the soul expanding, gone, whatever

the soul is or isn't, back to the woods at the edge
of the field above the floodplain & river – I hear it

in gobbler scratch, titmouse, riffle, and in between
where the snow promises to attend with a smell of

rust & rot, an old shell casing in dampdirt. I hear it
in the bark of the doe & the hoof stamp & leaves,

and see it in the sound of mufflers chugging inclines
on undistant roads, the hurt in cold fingers, snow turning

to slush, a stillness so active with flex & expectation,
as of something watching itself be watched by what

it cannot see only smell, motion's seedtime, prelude
to leap. Here the guineas have landed on shed roof,

their feet percussing tin, voices gasketless, pistoning.
Both loins in the cooler, I look east to ridges wearing

winter in gaps where leaves once blocked the light,
and am blessed along some axis of decomposition

and growth, slaughter being birth as birth is slaughter,
and I want loving meat to be a way to love & prey

on all generations – deer, acorn, mineral, soil, so on:
every quiver & twitch & hunter, road crossed, browse

and bloodleap, antler, ovary, hair, ear. I want to love
with belief in the shock & terror & hurt of the bullet

when it shattered rib, flooded lungs out of course,
the choke & stumble & longing, candle's last wax,

cold reckoning, last doe bred, unbred, scent of estrus –
and to have no knowledge of bullet's source, of bullet,

hunter, how much passion & hope in the body taken
and the body of the taker and those provided by

giving of take, savoring ground quarters in burger,
shoulder steaks with plum sauce, slices of heart,

oaky meat leavened by juniper berry, cumin, black
and red pepper. Last August we crouched by the fire,

turning a loin on the grate, hickory a sunrise of coals,
the kids wearing their hula hoops like Saturn its rings

in the photos anyway, Purgatory Mountain framing
our view to the west, calling our eyes as any giant

to see what we saw best because we didn't know
we were, only some curiosity to come or that was

in the spectrum of our togetherness, friends who
in silence or talking say so much more just

by being there, braces on a house when only the walls
are up, two outside walls, the nails in the braces

not the force or the motion that drove them. I mean
there we were, in the yard, two couples, kids, &

these deer, a herd of like eight, mosey into the field,
and damn if we're like even there more by such

presence – witness might be the word – or motion,
always that, the emotion of watching and the motion

being watched for is that being, this continuum, nobody
but a vibrating, throbbing tremor & that be us? – yup –

I'm cutting the fish from the chest cavity, the underspine,
one hand on sidemeat, holding it like one who when

handling wood tries not to know what the tree said as
it fell, these inner loins coming out, the fish as they say

around here, being the size of a good smallmouth or brown,
three to five pounds: I'm sketchier at guessing weight

than framing a window or door & to say killing deer is
essential to the health of our farm and land in general

or the herd, to say the word blood sport applies, to speak
of the thrill of the chase and so on ad mausoleum is

not helpful when both hands are having trouble steadying
the buck's rear quarters so as to remove them from

the wood that runs through the incision between tendon
and bone – these suckers are heavy & I'm not scrawny,

and the other night I was sleeping in the leaves where
the prior evening a deer had lain to rest or sleep, whatever

they do, when from the dream I woke to my daughter
in the next room coming down hard out of bed for

a cold trek to the bathroom, and I followed to detour
and load the woodstove then step from the side door

to the porch where I saw in three quarter moonlight
an inch of new snow bright on the land, and I stood there

looking at the glow of it in the mist & half light,
and looking, too, at the view from the leafbed

in the dream along more leaves, ground level,
saplings, trunks, the cedars in the thicket in the hollow

beyond – once at a deer camp near Jump Mountain
I helped six men drive an old clearcut, which reminds me

how sitting alone or walking, three steps then stop
a while, stand, three more or two or four, cannot be

called passive aggressive. You see a gun in my arms
and the desire to shoot it, no matter how one stands

or with whom, is a form of lust, a fine, simple lust
that exposes the conifers' bulk more honestly

since it's not any longer the mass I see and how that
contrasts with the hardwoods on the ridge and sky

beyond, green on violet on paler violet, distance
and proximity & bulk, but the seams in that mass

and how not looking at the form in particular but
at the shape of the base for a silhouette, movement,

sight of a sound heard though unheard until seen,
looking at all & none of that by trying hard not to

look too hard and see by being the movement of eyes
along the music of it – funny how often the sky enters

the dance of the hunt since deer do not bed down there,
the sky to which I continually look, as if to refresh

the goggles, spell them from the land – could have
said deer – its multitudes & tricks, and relieve the brain

for a spell from differentiating stalk, shrub, deadfall.
The sky by promising nothing is a generous sight,

blessing me with its fathoms, its unattainabilities.
Like looking at the way a deep breath feels, deep

and easy breaths, body & thoughts the same thing,
time all over you & in you – not present, not past or future:

time with all its sacks of feed fresh from the grindstone,
time in the shed with the hindquarters, nice flanks & all,

but heavy too & it's get them to the kitchen time, where
the deer takes over again, tells us how and how not

to cut it and so how to think about the sky by being
sky for a while since the sky trims the membrane

and cuts chunks much faster and cleaner. Curious places
open their ports now, voyages of fiber & fluid,

though when we butcher hogs the drab, pink flesh
provides pleasure less of contrast & speed than look

at all this meat – the romance economic, turn feed to
sausage, bacon, loin, hundreds of stacks, five of us,

Tommy in charge, smoke from the fire under the boiler,
bad smoke, hair scraped, hog on a pole, entrails too many

for a bucket; sides, shoulders, hams, heads hanging
from hooks, all of it hanging overnight in a shed tight

enough to let the cold in and not the cats, mutts –
our movements in time with those who came before,

gathered to take in order to provide & feel provided for,
and feel pride in the closeness the taking & providing

spawns, the closeness of the labor and the grief
of the nothingness such labor, by spawning,

celebrates. It is a beautiful tired I feel after days
working like that, with sharp knives, clean tables,

the long division of bodies, not just the hogs but
our own & how conversation turns along the anatomy,

bodies within bodies disembodying, one of the many
and many of the one, cubes for the grinder, knife

a horizon line, a marriage of separation, protein, acid,
nerve, fat, Randy Travis coming through the jambox

for the third time, retired hacksaw of an antenna
in the corner because it's late, there's another crate

to grind, knives to clean, sharpen, a floor to sweep
before morning when we mix sage & other spices

and work fat into the lean with bare hands, heat
of bodies essential to taste (palm oil), slap a patty in skillet

to sample, get it right, root hog or die, as in the woods
the deer are doing what they do & to say they are

not as domestic as, say, hogs fattened in a pen
on feed made with soy shipped from Brazil

where grown in fields once jungle, and on pumpkins
leftover from the best holiday, & whey from making cheese,

and eggs & other scraps, to say the deer are different
is to say those who kill for meat are not the same as

those who stop by Kroger, check sticker for good price,
right date: it's one cut or another, cured ham or sausage,

indulgence no matter how you scope it, a skidmark on
the endless four lane where there's only exit & who knows

when & where the off ramps lead – there was a guy a friend
of mine knew who hitched an old Chrysler to his tractor

and hauled it to a place in the field where since the frame
was shot but not the engine, he'd use it as a deer blind;

but first time he fired the heat and was sitting there
in the driver's seat, driving the view of the tree line & meadow,

the sedan starting to warm up, deer so much in mind
he doesn't notice the cucumber smell through must

of running board's rust and fabric rot until the noise
under his seat starts up, aboriginal percussion, only

more terrifying as it's a nest of rattlers waking to warmth
in the springs and holes of the seat. Some exit, though

our exits are always the body's way of saying hello, check
this out now that is not over but spilling into this, this

being the way the body responds to the completion
of a cut, knife having severed the flap of blood taint

from the neck roast, red heap tossed in stack
of scrap for dogs – it isn't victory then but

a satisfaction closer to waking to rain after a long time
of dust & there's a skim coat of mist over the river,

you know there is without turning in bed to see it
out the window through the body of the one tangled

in memory as in motion, soft footsteps of our child
from the woodstove where she's dressed to kitchen

where she's headed out the door to free her birds
for another day of chickenhood. I know it's quaint

to say that cutting fresh meat is a journey that takes me
as far into the woods in the life of the deer as any walk,

each press of knife, give of flesh a ride through places
that live in the shape & essence of a life changing, bone

and membrane, because to be aware of such energies
is surefire to rob them of possibility, so I cut & chatter

with wife and daughter who cut & chatter, though
it's quieter than dogs on a near ridge barking at night,

even with the stereo playing early June Carter, voice
strident as the dulcimer & some memory trace of

a demo job, tearing a house apart sheetrock by stud,
plate, imagining the men who worked to assemble it long

before the mill shut down, stood abandoned until
the boutiques, restaurant, co-op, coffee shop opened

in the refurbished space of it. The ducks, meanwhile,
are tilling the garden, drilling the thaw with their beaks.

The remaining hogs till their lot. Clouds till. We till.
Thump of knife blade on cutting board, thump & tap.

Duck quack. Hog grunt. Guinea squawk. Deer bark.
The train heavy with coal along the James, bones

by the tracks. The wind from the west, combed by
Purgatory, bringing highway noise the way ocean

brings sounds of the moon to the beach; the noise
of cars & trucks – honk, downshift, rumblestrip –

is less travel or transport anymore than the end
of an era, the last fix, the straw bringing more air

than milkshake from the glass. Oil & water. Meat
parts from meat. We almost forget our foolishness.

Say knife is an instrument of praise, say sharpen it.
The wind blows harder these days, few trees

to quench it. Here is windy, thus the meat, &
I swim each day along these currents, grace

and anguish, joy & graze. Hear knife on stone.
Here June singing her rasp slicker than a mole's butt:

if ignorance is bliss, then I'm the nation's biggest blister.
The point is not to waste an ounce, to trim membrane

and leave the lean – the eye along that angle, hand
holding steady the handle bolted to blade. The heart

is in the fridge – I didn't eat it raw in the woods
sitting crosslegged by gutpile or mark my face

with its warm red paint. Heart & liver I plopped
in a bag – I think it said Walmart – and we'll

eat them cooked as right as we can cook them, strips
hot with butter & iron, wind blowing through the mouth

as we chew, wind traveling us through its shifts –
hard from the south in grove of young beech, dead

leaves clanging, now out northwest a hundred yards
downslope, something to do with the ravine, peaks

and ridges, microclimates, though as much to do
with the unnameable, the deer & not the deer, soul

of its browse. Archealogy. Rewind. Pause. This, too,
is the hunt. The deer has multiplied. Kirsten chases it.

Sophie chases it. It wants to stay together and resists
attempts to steady it for the next slice. I think of men

who fill large trucks with deer gathered from roadside –
asphalt-smeared, fender-battered – and wonder if they

don't come soon, these luggers, to seeing the damage as
the life, energy of impact, speed & steel & bone. Soon

but not too. Or only. The way or the why or the and of.
Says J, helping B heft a big doe off the shoulder

where 81 dips from Purgatory to cross the James, You
see the game this weekend. And B is thinking how

he could have spoken more kindly that morning
with his daughter & wife. There are pieces the vulture

know better than life – how else surf thermals. We adapt.
Accidents do not speak to the death of the accidental.

Luck is J's boss saying no worries to his hacksaw
on the dash for cutting antlers. He cooks a stock of them,

takes a shot of it doctored with cayenne & garlic
each dawn before firing his truck for the drive

to the yard. The damaged fender is luck and luck
that we have Ziplocs for storing meat in deep freeze,

zipper Ziplocs so when I pinch, as now, my finger
in the seal while squeezing the air from the chamber,

what air will go, and sealing the thing, too – trying to
be fast about it too fast – it's all I can do not to shebang

the whole eat of raw, and plastic, too, wife & kid like
get a grips Popsicle. I like the latissimus dorsi, flap

a wing that never formed, though my daughter's hand
seems too small to be holding a knife like that, blade

the length of a bottle of something too good not to be
finished right now. Anatomy's a cookbook, how

the origins of a cut says what & how to do better than
nearly dying from love says what the Bible says. Pepper.

Dark fruit – plum, persimmon, fig. Muscadine, M80
of a grape. Watching her carves me continually to when

the deer was there after not being there, wacky way
to be & see, and no less wacky for being true. She

doesn't always cut away from her chest, too,
which freaks me out, but her eyes, hands say she knows

the price of her materials, that mast & pain come
to this for now & for later flopviscous on

the maple block, back & forth: this work brings life
to her dolls (you see we must be quiet when

they're sleeping); and there's Kirsten late in the era
of comforts, doing her best Cassatt, slicing, trimming,

letting the meat lead her knife as the knife her hand,
some work on both ends, both ways, the rut

of the wrist & estrus of the blade, for to cut is
to break down not break it down one time but

again, rumen to reticulum, leaf & bud to bolus,
cudstuff, the cellulose to carbohydrates — omasum

and abomasum, a four chambered affair, plus
the caecum, posterior fermentation vat. You know

down the pipe is never just down the pipe – it's
digestibility, body making scents of sense, nature

and nurture, fatty acids where earlier the mist
gathered on the leather & lance of rhododendron

escalatored, loud with symmetries. I mean she's cutting
the shoulder into chunks for the grinder, to worm

ground lean – tricep, deltoid, extensor carpi: later
in a skillet with green pepper & cherry tomatoes,

edge habitat of herbs & spices, scoop it on basmati
soft with meat bird stock – the meal of a mind

working cud of life as life's leaves allow. Meal
of crowshadow on oak trunks gray in coming rain,

clouds over Purgatory, clouds over Cove Mountain,
some derivative of mist on the air. Senses muzzle,

the body loads, thinks by being as being is touch,
as some meat it seems likes the blade & doesn't

sever but separates as though it needed that,
and the knife tells the hand this with ease of motion,

flux between befores; how a deer leaps from standing
a ten foot fence, flex & lean, is mindmeal, thought

giving chase & chasing, less leg than lightning,
trigger & powder, spark & fire, that by hiding right

exposes the hidden, water underground, microbe
and neutrino seep-bound or piped as at the spring

below Purgatory along Frontage Road, cress in ditch,
cider bugs, cans, the cold water some tongue not

of glass but shattering condensed, breathing's afterword;
some go for that hogwash, too, life becoming a trial

to reign the mind's wild water, channelize it, canal
the stray stuff, make it navigable, simple, a means

to transport the goods, though no good now the flow
that flew soon unflighty, currents with a dim pulse

of former energies. A matter of form and form
the function forming. Junctional. Dew claw.

Melatonin. Pituitributary. In the out of whack,
crouched, & the next step feeling to stop

before the crack of the stick. We think, we stalk.
To feed is to lose a trail as roots in soil the mouth

and the desire for mouth to let the body gnaw;
chewing, after all, is sloppy butchery – crockery –

and the deer's low trajectory into the extended
suspension phase of stride conserves energy

not so I can chew it like this or else so, I no
know, a zoo in here, more meat stacked

and cut or to be cut than in our bodies – it's scary
all that life & none of it whining about its needs

or even using the whining as a way to understand
them. If inert, so inert. Touch the whitetail's coat

in winter's pelage, grey of fullessness & deciduous,
and something in me molts, days lengthen, my nouns

forget they're words, goes molt & not because
it's soft or dead to purpose & alive to another,

though that surely fires me up – it's the moment
the fingers feel what they've touched, and the mind

what the mind feels just then, watershed of miracles
going batshit, a thing dead another living, removed

from geography of tissue & vessel, organ & bone.
The violation is thrilling with intimacy just then.

The intimacy violates. And I feel bad, love to,
real bad, a guiltshame machine, and then, suddenly,

sexy as hell – it's real this is the deal but not all
the time the wave's face bumps me, blade slips,

maybe a nick, blood on blood. I like canals, too.
Drifting, going nowhere. And the way the touch

touches to the moment where moment gallops
into & through & intersects as in a warm river under

a cold dawn, the way when I'm happy like this
it seems creation says what's up, whatever we mean

when talk goes to creation, say the spine of a book
by an old friend you've never met & know even

better from pages where black, little shapes
live like fur on a deer's coat, the deer we are & aren't,

the one buck that when it rubs we know the smell
of the bark tearing as it knows the chainsaw sound

and clatter afterwards, warm & tired talk of friends
cutting wood, some loblolly scrub pine hybrid,

for logs to build a playhouse for the kid, one now
slicing membrane from brachiocephalicus. Sure,

the cosmic was always a good standby. If life
is for asking what life is for & why we're here,

I want to know what is here if not the station
where pinecone is barkshape, broomstraw

is copper, and the dry creek speaks best of
the journey to bring all rivers together because

it is here & busts not a little shove of association,
the way over the hill to the southeast where the wind

so rarely comes from but often goes, there's a grove
of sycamore & paw paw below the old canal lock

between Buchanan & Arcadia, and paddling
by that place it is fine to feel the thick wall of ridge

on east bank nudge what sense of safety westward
where the floodplain opens and the field above it,

Stinnett's land, pine grove, hardwoods & the field
above that, the flat one then pasture on the ridge

over whose peak sits Old Man Trail's bunker of
a rancher & he in there smiling and lonely just dying

to tell of logging days, chestnut trees going down,
and daughter Lithia-way, for his memories of this place

become the memories footering the past being lived
as on this night we hunker by chopping block as worked

as working up lizardly cuts of lean, eighteen avenues
of desire intersecting with numberless in our bodies

even as we rock hard on the saddle of being together,
talking about what we never say – simple affairs – fetch

of eggs in henhouse, dog in heat, her fleas, firewood heap,
stovepipe needing another plunger of steel brush on

fiber pole bending behind while straddling roof peak,
trying not to fall in limestone chimney wild with clouds

moving like scum we skim from stock as it simmers
in steel pot just 19.95 at Walmart last week. Possibly

it fucks you up to take apart so many bodies – four deer
a year, a few hogs, chickens, ducks, sea trout & redfish

from Mom's fish market in New Bern, shad from March runs
up the Neuse – since mysteries of flesh & its containering

become uncontainered with all the breaking, chopping,
munching: let me nibble your neck roast, sweetie, I say

to Kirsten not all in jest as she stiffarms & giggles at
foolishness & love like a parasite inscoring bone &

pheromone. I have to play like that because the way
the deer fell & I sat for a few minutes with stomach acid

gnawing savage lovely swirl, water we drink more
than navigate, dig for more than drink – you know

how snow comes first on a gauze of air heavy with wet,
aluminum taste in nose, animals daisical in their orbit

from bedding place to feed to browse to water, so on,
before release comes as though arrival were old news,

the flakes having been there in mind, body, sticking
where temperature allows – warm to it or don't,

the stuff seems shaved more than blossoming, though
any origin spiel will do, it's night & the dreamless sleep

a ship on a bay of dreams, each flake a phosphorescence,
ground a wake off nightbreath's stern – the deer smell it

in taste of sapling buds, in cud & ungulus, pili erector
and incisor, gluteus & tine – and we sense it most

in muscles of fingers, all connectors along that interstate –
loco & motive – that steady the meat & work the knife,

so why explore the way a life can transform, as if in
the body, from eating what's in the store to the woods

and you're going in them with intention to take being
the store, start of it, there being a hopscotch of worlds

now to then to now, including in those chalklines a will
to flee that brings that which is flown from all

more present & unreleased in a releasing stasis where
the hill behind the barn becomes the shape of the shin

below the bent knee of the leg that knows nothing
of knowing & is better meniscus & tendon for it. There

is thrill equal in full sail of white tail, rump patch, sudden
– to my ear – pressure in ground coming through, air

of hooves exchanging flight with landing, collarboneless
quartering & eighthing, a slalom through oak & ledge,

slope & drainage, freakish illusion of trees making way,
ground settling, that pronounces you man & animal,

pursued & pursuer by joy of coming to this moment
more radiance than moment, world stamping its forefoot,

scents released, kitchen in dusk of constituents fussing
a fussed over, promiscuous ravishment of collisions. It's neat

how the silence of a deer moving at dawn through scrub pine
to leap fence at northern border where consciousness

has focus forever out of the sights is the silence of a child
humming an old carol while the news coming through

the radio says nothing of the news on the table where
she's exposed another gland, bean of a thing, & Mama's got

the tochanter major looking like niblets of mollusk meat.
But neater how silence is allowing quiet's bounty run of

the place, but not too neat to admit I'm feeling
good falling through what's never found with you

my knife dear ones cutting up the making. Listen past
black capped chickadee, past hawk & crow & wind in

what leaves – tool & musk know death is life but less
of how tendons flex when I think how much more

the deer know about themselves & my trying to know
what they cannot say only do – the wind is my guide

between the end & beginning, and after that it is light,
and wind & light, like thought & feeling, are not

always sincere. For instance, this morning in
the fuzzy time before dawn I walked the drainage

where boxwood does the shag by the sinkhole
and outcrop, and the wind out of the northwest

but at the top of the drainage where four ridges
come together to form five drainages & a larger ridge,

the wind was out of the southwest – dawn was
to blame. And the pressure ridge was to blame.

Blame, at it's best, is a hunt for origins, the nature
of the nature of the nature of feeling the wind

on your cheeks & walking towards the scentlessness
of those leaves underfoot even as the living, as it must,

takes you away from them, they from you. Dirt
was always the final turning after & on the page –

therefore I want to know what it says to deer hoof
when deer hoof & we, deer & tree & elsemulch is

what's said. I saw a car the other day, a Jeep
tricked out in full camo, the hard top (removable)

had stickers of deer, big bucks & makers of gear
all over the tinted glass, and I followed off the exit

at Troutville, then to a house where it parked so
I kept going, fueled by fantasies of meeting the driver

in the wilds of some geekout in warm weather &
he's wearing camo sunglasses, camo flip flops, camo

tank top & shorts, and there are tattoos of deer heads,
bucks, trophy racks on his legs & arms & neck,

and I say "You like to hunt," and he looks at me like
he's growing hackle, pretty stuff, before he says, "Yes,

I'm looking for a camo thong." "For you," I ask, but
he ignores me so I say to the cocaine-pasty sweetness

who works the place, "Do you have any sexy cotton
menstruation pads," and she says before she knows,

"No." And I say, "In purple?" Something vacant
about watching deer, boring animals – most –

skittish, ravenous, too thin & desperate to believe
that earnest look of joy chorusing the air, ennobling

somehow the whole ill world to seem healthy
beyond medicalspeak – vacant the way fidelity

to the home range makes the place full of zilch –
chop, chop, slice, slice: I'm never going to get on

the Seneca Depot in the Finger Lakes of New York
to see what the woods boil into when ghost deer stand,

black eyes tripping albino traps, but it'd be neat,
and who knows how big butcher downstairs

cuts the meat, how we're cooked. Geography
is distance & it's not the place but what you see,

the way it's less what you see than the difference
between how you see what you say about it

and how you say what you see when you're
saying it some futures before – look, those words –

saying it – are yellow, they're fast, they tear. I like
rot, its growth, how mushroom & moss in the dirt

through your fingers smell the saying it. Foxes
live there, too, &, too, their prayers have been eating

good scabs as long as night's space heaters have
been clouding over. Yellow & running through it,

tails up in alarm at you cutting towards yourself
repeatedly, fingers as close to the blade as necessity

is relative at this stage in the history of the world,
world being bluebird word, the the mist that could be

woodsmoke on a morning after a long, bright moon
spasticizing the night's unsleeping, time the arc

of source across the swerve, angle, shadowlay,
the view from perch fifteen feet up hickory that sways

slow as its roots, pudendulum & leaf, crickle & reap –
winter's swill, though at times the wind tiptoes, brothers

and sisters hiding in holes in trees. I pay allegiance,
I wipe my nose, see hands, boots, longings, hates,

cloudpudding dragging lavender avenues in
penultimate's penultimate dusk – the body comes

apart, sight breathing, breathing hope skimming
the curds of rapture afraid for a while to jump in; o

duty the fling answer when she calls the stillness
your name, but when the stickers & tats disresemble

tribal instincts or million tined mounts shrunk to
adhere, lid the widemouth for the deer know

each tree by names you taste best when cooked fresh
over burning wood, coals winking in gratitude's memory

evangelical as Gospel of Good Yolk Get Out! –
I mean the leaves where goings are comings as

the limbs earth's crazy stitchery, how voice is taste &
it's food that's love & work making food to love

that won't save us & save us, some lick of blessing
in its origins. Greed is tricky. As many ways to see

as ways to keep a muzzleloader's barrel from fouling,
as needles on pine limbs in the goat pasture – there's

no spectrum, no black & white this or else that way
to reduce it to the voice of a friend offering something

generous over the telephone – lonely, too – while
you stand on the porch cordlessly, somewhere aware

of animals sniffng your noise – ducks in okra stalks,
guineas on hurricane fence, barncats shriekling in spar

near tractorshed, deer in beeches hearing the smell
of extinction's pinfeathers. How long can this last?

This may be months from now, stench of creosote
on the hands. I don't know. Deer in freezer then,

burgers in taste bud memory. Gun cleaned, oiled,
and set aside – hid – ammo out of sight where days

their length & slow to green, more than rouge
on ridges, those broom factories, barbers of light

styling. Is to wander some dark roads towards
the darkness where sparks begin & the meat

caresses a comedy of tenderness in the wrinkles
of your hands, to cut, is silence before there was

a word for stillness either, or empty. Threads
where thread congeals. Things exist to move

from thing to thing & never just through mouth
or other breakdown machinery – to sever is to see

each tree in the forest giving truth some good lip
& truth all shucksy & so forth, dabbing its napkin

at bloodclots unsightly, not helping the meat lose
its freshness any beworsetter than comparison

places the stone on the mantle instead of sakes
where such keeps do not succeed in staying

from looking cluttered, thank goodness, though
they are all that tangle your spool, then some

more than sum, I mean that's where it's going,
essence of underkill, always not having enough

and having to term with that by fictions & myths
& nondismythifictional journeys – lies, mostly –

the way that bucket of scraps – coffee grounds, peels,
husks, drainsplooge – is not saving the world by

going to worms in bins in hothouse, all plastic
and southfacing, a late last late winter affair that

looks cluttered & crashedkitelike blistering off
the south wall of the cinderblock shed – golly, you

should smell that den of improprinquity when
goat & chickendung cook in; it grabs your trachea,

wrings out all the warblers of reduplication. Worms
can have their modularity & table scraps & feed

our chickens that stuff in their stuff when time,
as when next train grumbles along the James full

of corn, other grains – we won't Jesse James it,
drop a tree or two, hop boxcar, load sacks

and then get back – yeah right, too much work
for a life that's words going to the horizon of

the horizon of the horizon of the event within
the mutations, hazardous & stray, purity's blank –

what the mind says when the brain is frying eggs
where the eyes used to, those opticals then, from

and into soil ravenous to its leastmost. It's late fall.
Deer, like the days, made larger in their smallness

by long nights. A journey of breath where footsteps
no less than the path to nowhere is being, lost in

service to an applebutter dusk. Charitable days:
small acts, winter readier than we know with

its fusty cloak – hay losing its juice in barn, meat
playing notes on the knife we'll hear as fusions,

taste's phrasings spilling the guts of a dream
your mother never told you she lived, giving lyric

the okay to get ahead of itself, a nanosplurge
of dirt, lead, air. No, nothing like tripling back

on something like this slug of membrane that
just slid on the floor under my wife's shoe. "Work

is loss," she doesn't say. And I don't say the bit
about loss in accumulation being dust on the gain

by the sacrifice – life's life when somebody talks
smack about somebody else by talking about

nobody but himself. Snelled, we're hooked,
a full creel, crutch & refleece, water through

the wicker. To want to know less about deer than
the deer do poses a problem – what kind of freak

would say such a thing when there's a kid
in the room explaining the reason we don't need

another reason for wanting to live another life;
whittle & twitch, she's going hard at socket,

some pale globule of cartilage putting the word
for smooth to shame, and it's walking me across

the pasture thin from last haying as shadows bend
another fifteen essences under ridges where

laurel hocks wind's dulcimers for chump change,
though the grouse could give a hoot with

a beakful of coralberry, other seeds. The body
knows best when given to the body that will be

its own – death is figurative – what we eat how
we inhabit the life after this one, after that who

can say the way a forkstab of loin bequeaths
an inheritance one doesn't hurry to spend. I cut

into the pasture along the fence & enter the woods
that I'll never know so as to hunt owl-like by

sound in the dark: the new savage was always
old news, but tonight I sit against a big red oak

and listen to listening's glistening conjuring dew
that by dawn'll be frost, igloos of mist, the sun

over Bedford County before it crests Flat Top
and spills its chest on us, needy as the job & roof

and wheels – simple wealth not often enough,
therefore wealth. Tonight we're rich with proof

of heavens no closer, further than blood, meat, bone,
tools for render, storage, and the problems we call

our own seem very small, and the face of nourishment
many faces – words hurled, lodged to bone, they're

something to laugh about & in laughing share
a song beneath the voice & the throat that chants

remember this – whatever else you may do, that
does you – do not forget the one body we are most

in the gathering of bodies around a gift – I don't say
earned – of slaughter that's fresh enough our

walk seems as much a means to preserve & store,
put by for good meals across seasons as motions

to preserve the spirit that speaks in the hush of
the knife's course across & through the flesh,

an act not distant from the photographic – art,
I mean – making something that exalts in making

and in the made; it is like the rain in mind that
patters a balm & becomes thinking simple, coursing

the lowest ground, turning on itself in uncoursing
of that course, becoming not new or old but worn,

gravity-sinuous, a silent negotiation, a lucidity.
The wrists ache, fingers hurt to grow wings, fly:

let them go, the bodies so soon to be soil, with
the body of a kitchen in blossom a pollination

of pieces becoming more, strip, cube, chunk —
the coffeemaker not less from the carnage, how

we feel the year, nearing end, all its labors, again,
in this quiet, menial art, each trip to woods, woodpile,

sawblade, stove — the repairs of pipe & roof, additions,
rearrangements, purchases, sales. The buck, too,

has outgrown his coat. Sick, maybe, but not close
to ill. How like clouds the years of rain & hues,

all that difference in the same scene, so soon
the heat under seed starts, the weeds, barefoot,

vacuumy days, always the right amount to do
and not do in order to do something else. Done.

Rot. Blossom & leaf & young. New fawns by
the far fence lusty with touch as much as touch

can bear — each cut a kiss, kisses a hatchery,
tools entering the body that with heat & herbage

will enter us less as man enters woman than child
bends the minds of its makers in directions the

highest limbs refuse to mutter, even to sapsucker.
Meat is bread – a dough of tree, cloud, rock that birth

kneads & living bakes. We, too, are on the rise,
insighting the unseen. Knife, then, is blessing,

and we are not as living as we look, thus we look
and by looking live through that which is not

as unloving as it looks. See, trees no longer seem,
for a while, boorish in their majesty of bud & cull.

The ground where the buck fell was banked with leaf,
in places bare – some acorn – a roadbed long without

wheel, knowing travel, what news of the elevations
brings the leaves to stone as the loin of leap

and nerves to our tongues on some quiet
February day, water singing from the pot

on the woodstove, a fire harmony, a warmth –
is this how the thrush learns of warbler,

siskin? I think we are dying well here among
all this life. I think therefore I am not. I cut

and am blue giving birth to red, red to gentle,
gentle to bone, rawest meat. This is flesh

made word, and if I'm lucky the butterflies
of it might be enough to season an experience

akin to living in & after the game, gathered &
gatherer, flank, ear, tine. Base alchemy,

leaf of flesh of dance. We true the walls of food
along the pitch where desire & duty define

the degrees, a geography of intimacy. Home
takes root, walls sturdy with attention, a front

scraping its knuckles on the roof's north valleys.
We are breathing limestone, mapping the caves,

where the water comes from when it goes
underground. Nature is taking us apart. We hoard,

throat, almost rhyme with root. I want the truth
to stop dreaming for a change as every last scrap

of lust enters the meat through small acts, and smell
the smoke off the cuts on the grill in June, limbs

from a pruned peach lending Ozymandiac breath,
but I can't see the scene for then I'm seeing the three

of us bent over what is & isn't fun or work or even
recipe for a good night's leap; there's no meaning

to this, there's virulence & plenty. If compassion,
if distance & delight, if fondle – it blazes less orange

than eclipse. What are we not if we are butchers?
Nothing's left out of use here, thus our stomachs

learn such discrimination that we feel mortared
by the usual, even fine restaurant fare? In kitchen

does live devour at its daintiest; in these knives
it's nothing. Here we are, the path along the paths

the knife doesn't take, and there are a couple
of eyes walking that way real good & slow with

a sort of inner eye for seeing the schism within
the deal, I mean there's a map beyond the end

of geography & that is the way of the deer. See
the ribcage next year in the limbs, hooked there,

just off the chicken yard, less a totem than
a next time when time is out for a bite. I'm always

thus unspelled by this chore, always a little less
translating from living language – deer – to

the deadliving language – meat – and from meat
to the lifegiving language of cook, and from that

to eating: there are times I wonder if I see so many
more deer when I'm hunting morels, hepatica,

trout lily, out following the trace of a hunch, cruising
the timber, so to speak, kicking around where

the wind is least, carried by the promise of shadows
and how cresting a ridge or rounding the bend

of a tree the end of a hunch may trace the start
where middles the instance of dismemory – look,

we're making wholes of wholes, deer within breathing
beyond eye's reach. We slice days at the pace of

the care of animals, plants, feed & housing, groundwork,
the deer at the margins, aware of each of us by smell.

Among the orchestral flocks, we cut our tiredness.
We cut at the cut before the cut to come, cut at

the ancient language of a knife in the hands going into
the meat of animals whose voices inhabit our own even

more than the meat in our mouths some evening some
season from now. Well, sort of. Getting it done

is not the name of the game, in other words, but
the name the game changed into wristache. If

the winter woods are a kind of diagram for
exhaustion, all the inexhaustible lives, like roads,

the eyes drive – and the feet at times follow – the deer
that appear across the pastures of your looking

in passage to another task, a glimpse become
a holding pattern in which through the visual

the body recharges as if fueled by the course
of the task (because walking to the chicken house

is as much a part of feeding the chickens as dipping
the old Folger's can in the grain bin) (because

the chickens must at a level beyond knowing,
fantasy, know in their gleam the pulse of the body

that carries their cracked corn) – the deer then
are dirty, radiant conglomerates of all the exhaustion

has filtered forth, alive & breathing and so ready
to flee for thicker, safer cover the eyes of

their beholder sees those places, too, lives there;
and I remember beyond memory at the sight

of four does at dusk by the north fenceline
where the big pine fell in the last big wind,

and the memories along that tangled path spark
a discordance of voices, places, smells, as when

earlier this fall I made enough extra cash to buy
my first nonmuzzleloading rifle, so I sniffed among

the buds & found a gunshow & a couple of makes
and models that seemed with proper vintage

affordable, and I'm telling my buddy this & he says
wait, let me make a few calls & ten minutes later

he says meet me at the gas station, so I do & we visit
a modest home where on the kitchen table among

some real heinous, dayglo stuffed animals rests
a lever action for less than I'd bargained for,

and the crewcut selling the piece doesn't let us leave
without taking three cartridges because "selling

a gun with no shells I might as well be giving
you a river rock." It is quick, the insemination, when

a buck mounts a doe. True love ends in death
that keeps ending in life. They clucked & choughed,

the squirrels of the woods where my childhood
is a speck of paint on a dirty window, and when

I dropped the first one with a pellet to its forehead
just over the ear, grazing it, even then the world grew

simple all of the sudden, as if sudden had roots
in forever, and I went to school – 3rd grade – and

I sat among the teachers learning from what
they taught how not to learn from what is taught,

and then I came home where Dad when he came home
changed into something casual and skinned & gutted

the no longer soft, gray lump that knew each morning
by the quality of the light on its hole in the oak until

that dawn when the kid who sat behind the roots
of a windfall turned him to stew meat which Mom

fixed up real well. Always we cut into ourselves when
we cut meat taken from land not our land because

we pay the bank each month to say so, though
some say so, but because our thoughts & bodies

are mulched by our mulching it: cut wood for stove
& wood cut splits many ways day's grains & time

splinters along the contours – pasture to woods to ridge
to ridge in distance undistancing as near becomes

known as the back after a day hauling one thing
alive or once alive to another way to burn. Along

even closer contours – in the mouth, for instance,
and in the spiders in the shed & the shadows

of the spiders cast by the bed of coals in the spine
the color of the taste of that Total Insanity Hot Sauce

on Judy Nelson's smoked venison stew packed
with yummies she knew from the home range, being

who we are when who is a feeding habit more than
more or less. Look, movies don't cut it. And the books,

many books, are a taxonomy of computer farts.
I want good ground, good cover. Walking the range

in pitch dark & knowing where you are by the feel
of the ground under bare feet, flex of ankle. What

the knife says & the meat in return. I want to be
in pieces like that, and the pieces in places where

the better pieces scramble more than wholes through
the center of every now being severed from the next.

The drift gets you one way or other, bloodrift, lifedrift,
deathdrift. Even now, as we laugh & chat & listen to

to listening's chatter & song, we cut into our conscience
as we cut into meat bloodless save for its making, blood

in us rising to being here, a small family trying to know
what we never can by simple measures, eating the food

that nourishes as a moon over a cold ridge alive with wind
and shadow, bud & limb & light, nourishes & guts us, too, in

the act of its gathering, in planning & prep, in brass,
sheath, gun oil that stares at & stirs you from shelf

where in passing I can't help but feel the weight
of parts coming together for the slowest walking,

mapping silence for movements that make sense
for a while the ladder of living, how by being top rung

I'm bottommost, & being so, glad the blood is gone, glad
there's a place in the woods made sinister & holy by

the stain; sometimes I listen to that cry from the ground
even if it's not, & it's not, crying for me or for moonlight

through trees, colder nights when rhododendron leaves
fold, cheap cigars, and the galax goes brittle like lakes

the ducks forego in favor of rivers, where the water
stays open places it moves the most, like us, orbiting its orbits

according to gradient & stones. The first fall in this place
I killed a doe at thicket's edge on a windy Thanksgiving,

one shot with the 12 gauge, slug entering under spine,
messing up the tenderloin but dropping the deer hard

for a death that's never quick enough, as if to fertilize
the thicket at the heart of the game. I pass this spot often.

I wander the woods, end up there, the place with moss,
running cedar, deadfall, trunks as a meteor brightness

unlooked for yet seen in body as in sky. Last year, when
the season of rut gave way to hard ground, snowfall,

a little more light each day, seeds to start, walls to true,
dawns of waterfowl, afternoons of greenbriar & laurel

and hopes to kick up a grouse, & books by woodstove,
gossip leaving the chimney in transpacities – river mist,

lingering drifts on north facing ridges, when all that got to
going on, I saw the places where the deer had fallen, began

with our work to spiral into us, and I could not unsmell opening
the belly, careful not to puncture stomach but spill the infinitely

finite interior, separating liver & heart for the mix – the rest feed
for scavengers & plants. I don't try to forget these times, hands

rank with filling, some collector upon a horse conch in finery
of spiral, curl, grace. To kill well means gutting & butchering well,

and eating even better, with gratitude & pleasure & sharing,
and though the hunt, weeks & years of living these moments

in waiting & practice can be satisfying to the point of dangerous
without a kill, the murder is all the more honorable to all involved

woods, family, animals – by care of its finality, and yes disgust
is essential to that care, disgust, revulsion, fascination. Things

turn tropical then, trapezoidal. I have seen the thicket in
the eyes of my daughter when she's telling me something

that moves her, like this a.m. she says there's a surprise (cobbler)
in the kitchen, that her milk goat Fidelma is getting over

her cough but is still limping; how she & Ki ground a hundred pounds
of layer mash with Tommy though his Fyce hound Pickles

raised his leg against one of the bags – the thicket & not
the deer, thicket as much the deer as deer is ticks & chickadee

in that briary galactica. Landmarks. Spine & stalk. Of course
there are great men who lure greater than themselves

to a private ranch in Montana for an out of season trophy kill –
some overendowed mule deer buck or elk they want only

to do with a trigger-pull & ornament of antler for some room
in a house made sad by people for whom living is a flight

from life and therefore a life closer, perhaps, to the deer
than I know. Danger is an overdraft fee. The banks erode.

My knife dulls. I dance to the swipe of its edge on stone.
Steel is meat & meat stolen with careful ritual is

less stolen than a transfer of funds, accounts so far
abroad & of no account – such men are thieves & fools

and I love thieves & fools for their examples of who
we can hope not to be but are in ways known as the body

knows radon oozing from the crawl or the orgiastic,
mind-ballooning freakout that in moment of separating

the lungs & liver & heart from the trachea the hand's care
in the chest cavity may or may not quell. Such men,

trophy sluts, do not poach, do not run with deer or wolves
any more than in long days the leaf juice fat on hide

and the signs on the fence, and though need may be
more arbitrary than a dominant buck's pattern, we give

our due where we do. We do not eat deer these days.
We do the broth thing. Do some rice, sauerkraut, roll

the tart out of the coriander seed against the gum. Sip
a Miller, knowing the High Life lives most in the low

even if it's getting late & Neil's singing from the jambox
about packing it in when our freezer can't hardly yawn

with its mouth full of Ziplocs fat with future meals,
little heavinesses of dawn sky clouding over – yet

there's another ham we won't saw for roast but unskim
the sheen of membrane, whittle fat from lean, lean

from mass in strips versatile for riffs on standards
in hot skillet and hickory fire time. I like to look at

the faces, each a body, as the knife invites another
couple to the scene, then another, each with growthsheds,

rays medullarying, face after face in expressions
encompassing more than I know that I know that

I do not see, the moving a picture of deer's life &
our own, conceptions copulating, the life in death

as the light & hunger for light in the oak's silhouette.
It was always like this: murder & grace share a seat

on the train and in the long tunnels under mountains
of reckoning strange deals are made, later to be filed

in the bone building vital fluids leaf through. Touch
is evidence, evidence deersay. I'm tired of needing

this intercourse, and in love with tired's cuts &
need's flavors. If tired – not weary – is putting God

in us, then let me say thanks through varnishes
of that motion – feel of legs still warm from the bed

in the last dark moving through the fencegates
and pasture edges to the briary edge, the saplings

with their cold caress, roughness on cheeks,
the gun's weight as it shifts as I duck & scurry

along the hypotenuse of quiet & noisy to places
that through gifts & signs the deer are apt to be

even in their absence, be as an expectation that spells
itself in tendrils of breath & the heart's flurries coming

through the coat, layers under the coat, but mostly
up the throat – no smell of blood only listening

for its bearings, ears as aware of the wind as trees
swaying with it, the buzzards turning on the feathers

of its swells, ridges unceasing, the songbirds squeaking,
a jay silhouetting against the sky's uncomprehension,

some solidity of emptiness & ascension as each leg
feels through the booted foot for least resistance

of weight. And then the next chapter of stillness begins
as the body moves towards the least movement, because

when I am stopped, the eyes & blood pick up the slack
and race along the traceries for that space when

the deer – unseen, unheard – is present as through
the nose, a vibration in the hairs between knuckles

of fingers glove – soft on barrel & stock. Times like this
I could argue with passion & little sense for the presence

of as many more senses as those we possess, as buck
has another besides taste & smell that sparks

like those do, urges & motions based on what script
of chemicals the machinery – pore, organ, nerve – in

the mouth's low roof reads after or as the buck licks
fresh urine from doe. His neck stretches, lips curl.

The tongue has a role, too, in what goes down
in the vomeronasal organ either side of septum.

None of it is very clear to me but I like the gist
and have seen small bucks pause by small trees

to lick, necky & uplifted as if about to wail;
deer we've nearly undone here did it as time

stretched with my waiting & hoping it would move
well away from or to a clean shot. The deer did neither,

and I sighted with my weak eye, shot righty clean
through the ribs that now in the chicken yard, attached

to spine, give goodness to hens. The days
are a marinade, each a marriage though not always

the loin. I like tamari, sea salt, thyme, working
with various meats, steel, wood, stone, ink.

In winter there has to be a stove & fire to fuss over,
finest heat save the body of one whose wants

known so long I know that I won't in sickness
or in health or health's essential sickness. I cut this meat

in order to feel the flight of a hunch which is
the motion of any wild thing and these woods

and hills, too, but mostly to eat. Well. Along & across
I swing & press the blade & songs begin that are best

for how they're almost heard. I look at Sophie
and see a child close to the distances between

what close too rarely means – somehow it all pushes
pause on the anguish song so often played,

replayed I wonder the nature of its can & nitrates.
Another time in a river flowing with rain I hung,

facing upstream, at the inside of a bend, waiting
to watch a pal dance his craft through the waves

and rocks whose whittling ran from my chin
when just as I saw him three deer appeared

midflight from the left bank & touched foreleg
to riverbed not far from the bow of his boat, launching

again just as his eyes unstitched another merit badge
from grace's sash. I love the unexpected most

when it rocks the known world of routine, as if
without routine surprise could even thrive, like forage

I suppose, and the herd and how the heat goes in
and out of you this time of the sun far away,

hard ground, no foliage for speed limit on the wind.
Does in groups along the roads in the dusk that

sometimes lasts all day. I need this cold sharpening
its knives on the trunks, bark the burrs on a bastard file –

all the damn clothes, boots, gloves, fingers chapped
past the point of uncracking. Ice in the shade on north side

and north side of that. Small things turning accomplishment
to stew meat. Balm of the forties, early afternoon sun.

The way the exhibits get reincurated in the bone museum
and sapyard. Peril & austerity. Indulgences of night.

The crow, the waterfalls turning from ice to ice. This
is the honest season. It's harder to hide now that hiding

is less willing to look for you. Screw all the knots
in the boards. Pattern is to repetition as spiral is

to iron chain, and if you open the latch to that one
you're coming down an old logging road on

a turkey scratch with the quiet wrapping you
in the skin of how little you thought of the life

you live, and how the wind in the leaves could
relate with that, cut after cut, vessel & vascularity,

smilax along the edges its own edges multivide:
say it's a narrow valley, steep-ridged, the other side

dappled with week old snow as if skidmarks
from the sun's lowriding, slow drag deal, and there

are small cedars rubbed to frayed in places,
and the squirrels have been digging, the ground

a mouth chewing the many mountains of its selves
into mountain, hitching a ride on runoff, boot, beak,

claw, and hoof, & though the deer you hunt
are elusive, the quiet you have to hunt first is

a practice as abundant in its kinship with leaves
and mist, so you're doubly fucked & it's fine,

a real delicate affair, better than beauty for the way
it enters through the expulsion of your pores – here,

spike your ear with smilax spine – the sky is coming
to rest in its fashion: death is in the light & life

in the shadows that touch your own growing longer
with the meat being raised to the power of the slice

of my daughter's knife, her hunt for the clean,
efficient way coming through the old songs

she hums to rain on her mouth's valley & ridge,
raising the rivers, silting banks, covering

the tracks so other tracks can flirt with the tense
of the new, which is now & unnamed despite the seasons,

something the weather cannot touch, a touchlessness
at the conception of the nerves, all ganglia, arterial,

trimmed from the lean because it's chewy, gets hung
in the teeth, taints the mouth's budmeat,

this lipid that once lived in the acorn's tenorus oils
and then in the deer as leap & heat & knowing, deep,

microbial knowing – poise & equilibrium – we bring
ourselves to the table in ways that open the distances

to manageable morsels, your oak tree, my backrest,
as the soft, brownpink crunch of your foot says here,

I am crowheckle, you the cedar's forked crown where
long after the meat has been cut & packaged, frozen

and thawed and eaten – mostly enjoyed – I will sit
twenty yards off, hunting for the hunt beyond prior hunts

in bark fray, squirrel chatter. It's not the moss that turns
the deadfall to life, nor the ridge's hard pillows on

the flannel sky where the rain sleeps far from
the sun's severity & ridiculous staring. Cut! Keep at it.

Let knives be puppets alive despite the hands;
they are dancing – your bone trimmer, my bulbous

dwarf sword. The limbs are far from the tree & too many
with their bark, say those who logged these woods, who

live in the haunts of the lack of understory. I want cover,
timber & vinesnag, creeper & laurel & boulders. Winter

with its gusty struggle for finality. The kitchen
that breathes the woods enters the stalk of the eye

through the limbs' telescoping geometries – not
all triangles, either – see, do not see, without looking,

the way one limb opens on the distant tree, there
turning here on its other there, a compression, all

the torn leaves, shards of acorn caps, cracked saucers
always holding the right lack of rain. Somewhere too close

to be visible a deer barks, futile alarm. Sucks the sky
some purples from the ridge. Things go both ways

of the both ways they don't go. How can we be closer,
a young family, to each other, to our ideas of each other,

to the weeds & plants the deer do & do not browse,
save through the necessary distances as when the wind

raises the leaves from the ground to make temporary trees
and scrub pines sway & rock in convulsions that translate

the language of laughter, and how when the meat parts
from itself & then from the knife in birth of gratitude

and steel, you have glanced through the window at scenes –
fencepost, copse, ridge, sky – that like a diamond stone turn

along glances & swipes, and quarter the mind according
to notes, electricities only the shade of a winter hollow

can explain. Later the robins & at a later later the redbud
and the creek on the rise. Deer with an a is when

in the midst of cutting meat, roomwombed, we turn
and touch, maybe big, a hug, buss, press of hips,

body saying what our words no longer – thanks
for doing this with me, for being the other side

of the blade on the knife that our union, even when dull,
is. Tell me what is more trifling than a knife however

sharp & strong & handmade that isn't used. Collectibles,
kiss my creosote – a blade is dead that doesn't know

the force of wrist guiding it along the resistances – rope,
wood, plant, meat. Days of doing are here again, here

if we choose to be done in the doing according to
closenesses known through motion. Fertility lives here,

along with death & dirty cloth napkins, the kid's first
sewing project. You know how it is when you step

in a kitchen or toolshed, how you know a person more
by the state of things than by anything spoken – the sun

doesn't set on a small thing rightly used & placed,
and there is a right & to know it & know its place

is to return from the depths of the forest and feel
those dilations immeasurable in bearings forever

standing us where we never stand long, breathing
with lungs of the lungs we fed the dogs, the trout's gills

the chickens eat when churn the dogwoods the butter
the morels under not only the poplar try to ignore

and are fried in, no matter if we ever find them –
it is felt – look at the last strips of the flank & you

do not know the womb but feel its membrane stretch
along the lines, if they're not scribble, your eyes ride,

composing the moments within moments slice
by slice, soaked in a past stronger than the past

you recall, if from photograph or shock or trying
not to, look along the paths of the deer in flight

from the scent of your not seeing, for the way
seem the trees to breathe their long necks &

stretch into the motion of sap & limbs configuring
in lust & buglove, yes & see what you see

if you see anything for long but a pelagenous blur,
sum of birdflight and landing and soil soiling

the stone the grit the pulp of rain rising & settling
along the veins & crush & flex of oak leaves

the reddish brown of knowledge becoming by
its disappearance less the fault of testosterone

in the plasma – the origins of cryptic are siderean,
you know – than the sun no longer hoisting itself

on the sky's neck. I've never understood
countershading, how the white of belly, lower jaw,

and undertail dispels the shadow of the body on
the ground, but I am trying to inhabit those shadows

even now in the kitchen as Kirsten slaps more
cubist renditions of flank into grinder tray &

our girl works the ground into itself, water
over rocks, & I pack the meat, sixteen ounces

to bag, bricking the substance formerly known
as deer – ghost of the woods, what have you – so

the air's gone, it freezes best that way, tastes okay
when thawed a day then palmed in patties for

a little party with friends when the days begin
to dilate and the deer live most in gray ridges

undappled by midmorning sun higher than the prior,
the clouds vertebraed over Cove Mountain,

a few jet trails; but now we got to get these bones
in the stockpot, some to dogs, the skin from the fence,

feed the hogs, chickens, goats, descend further into
the orbit of being fed, yes, clean this mess up

and down, get the kitchen, knives & hands ready
for another round – something light: popcorn.

MILK IN A PAIL

First Polly, with udder-heavy thrust, lifts
her hind legs on stand's base, taps across

and slips head through keyhole's transept,
wide spot, & down, neck, handsome neck, inside

so as to reach bucket wedged in deck &
then feed, Blue Seal's *Caprine Challenger*

for grub; & now Sophie who at thirteen
has been running this routine for five years

locks her in with bolt half through PVC
and half in red oak. She talks to the goat,

brushes her, wipes her udder, her hands, sits,
strips first milk to a bowl she places on ground

for cats; pail sterile & stainless soon under,
the girl's squeezing one teat, next teat (elbows

out), two thin streams alternating a rhythm
like breathing, fast at times though mostly

just right, white trailings, ear low on doe's flank,
mouth's quicksounds working feed from bucket

into throat -- birdsounds, bugsounds, babysounds --
sun under hardwoods now no sun now sun

through clouds over the cordwood stacked
by fence, woven wire, strand of barbed

at peak where the next does, munching cud,
wait at goat's curious pace. Meanwhile,

William & Ola, twin babies, wrangle in
the Pack n Play a frog's leap from milking stand,

and watch & don't watch but sense something
regular's going down, the way the udder

shrinks slow to shrivel after being so full,
bouncing from inner thigh to inner thigh

each time Ms. Doe trotted a bit – Polly,
Geraldine, Matilda, Nellie – good-uddered

Nubians, not the best breed for volume
but best for butterfat, sweet milk, good to

sip or chug or slug a bit to lighten the night
on a mug of darkbrewed. It goes like this,

the human herd grown, the other flocks
and herds more populous too – chickens, ducks,

goat kids, guardian dogs, lambs under ewes; yes
this spring – of newborns & whatintheworld,

of so much & time for it, & time so stretchy
and pinched – this spring we set up the Pack n Play

next to the milking stand in the graveled carport,
and even now – late summer – as I grip

Polly's legs so she won't kick the pail our
oldest's stripping milk into, I watch our babies

in the strange crate, that honeycomb of mesh,
playing a primitive polo with spatulas

and a felt ball, or swinging a little stuffed giraffe
by the neck, or chewing on the label

of some toy or other, chewing on their fists,
the other's finger or ear. They are cutting teeth.

Ola has started to wave & clap. William
likes using his feet the way monkeys do,

trying to, legs like dough that won't stop
rising. Crazy. Lucky. Yes, we have too

many roosters this summer but fine since
sleep's as rare as one clear thought. Kirsten,

her gardens are extravagant, thick & wild &
gaudy even with more perennials than trays

of vinegar fries served at the local carnival
for firefighters & rescue squad, the fair

with a two-headed raccoon & a sheep
with five legs, funnelcakes, Tilt-A-Whirl – know

the scene, parades of obesity, camo & Deere,
thick belts, heeled boots, a few downwardly

mobile, new rural-foodie types like us;
and know, too, how Sophie's been dealing

this summer since learning her two best friends,
sisters, 12 & 15, are moving away. Reads book

after book. Sews dresses. Learns another old
fiddle tune. Loves on her goats. Never mopes.

Now her corgi Caleb's licking the pink place
undertail of some ewe! Always something

these August mornings, Sophie milking,
working dark, hot teats over the stainless

while I grip legs, prohibit kicks & milk-
taint, soothe the twins & then move buckets

to kitchen to filter the milk into Masons
to get on ice in cooler in the room where

last week was spent cleaning a lye – for soapmaking –
leak. These endless mornings, I think they are

milking us too. Time's soupy these days,
soapy. Time on the telephone watching

a praying mantis stalk a little butterfly
on the green expanse of a hosta leaf. Time,

predator & prey. Pray. You're darn right
mantis got a meal. Time, milky time. See,

Echinacea's pink tentacles began
to wilt mid-July this summer. We grill.

On locustwood, cedar, oak, & maple.
Goat chops – chevon & cabrito – & lamb chops,

lamb & beef burgers. Onions & squash, peppers,
potatoes. Two accordions, Sophie's hands –

Polly's teats: fingerflesh, fingerflex:
mammarianflesh. Polly, Geraldine, Matilda,

Nellie – each morning Sophie does this dance
with, & we dance on the edges, Kirsten,

William, Ola, & I. A dance desirous
as needful, as yummy to make as to drink;

arias of bleat, trilly & plaintive,
the goatcoat's shine, molasses & honey,

pale at knees & underbelly, at udder
and nose, ghostshapes on flank & crop,

rump & chine, no two coats the same nor
bleats nor milk nor temperaments. If

husbandry, more wifery, the stand brought
from the milking room at the barn, the barn

too far & complicated with twin babies to
tend to. Weeks some goat's eyelids show pale

so Sophie gives shots, drenches, treats for
parasites. Ducks & chickens chase bugs. Nothing

is endless & the days go on forever.
Kirsten makes chevre, yogurt, fromage blanc –

works the milkmagic with the goatgoods
and her own, for twins, while off the front porch

a broody duck sits under maple in a shady cove
of perennials, & stretches her neck & hisses

whenever person or dog approaches. We watch
her mornings while pushing a baby or two

in swings we hung from a good limb there.
Broody stares. We stare. Sometimes she moves

a stick or chunk of mulch around, tidying
her very tidy nest, & maybe we glance south

to goats browsing sidepasture – they often face
away from the sun – the curve of their back

the arc of Purgatory Mountain, long spine
to the west, western rim of the bowl

we live in, the rim we live nearest to,
that feels most container-like. Nights we sit

in the glider, moon nearly half-mast
or more – the moon has felt large all summer,

as though it forgot how to wane or its shadow ran
out of juju, or milk was moon condensed, pulp

of lactose, fat globules, nitrogen – none visible
but felt in digestion, in how it goes down

and what the body does with it & what
the days, all the doohickory, do with the body; yes,

albumen, too, & minerals: calcium, phosphorous,
chloride, copper, iron. We sit & let eyes fall

on some burdock & some lightning bugs & some
gauzy upwelling of a treeline north

of here & a little east, east being
to north as seeing to thought, barnroof

to rainfall, moccasin to rattler. One fang
or two, we learned this summer not to apply ice

to the next snakebite since the Wagner's oldest
got copperheaded at the Preece's cookout –

ice leads to tissue damage. Burdock talks
as it grows, mocks me for not digging deep

enough when plucking it – stuff spreads like
cigarette butts in rocks when the tattooed,

sideways-ballcapped crowd the swimming holes
at Jennings Creek. Take your compost out,

says burdock & then says it again. Or was it
get your babies on a schedule. Something in roots –

a fenceline, a shore. Cantaloupe, watermelon,
flypaper. I don't know. Sophie knows, yes her

grip's got that intermammary medial groove.
I'm holding Polly's ankles, Sophie her teats,

and looking down the driveway through red maple
to catalpa in the big pasture's lowplace –

shackling & shackled, how holding is to be held
if not accountable then hopeful, or close to it

as the wails, the shrieks, teething fits like
little seizures. Twinbabies. William, Ola Rose.

Quivering cheek, arms, lips. Love's quiver,
how milk is motion, motion touch – basket

of ligaments, balanced: pelvic symphonics,
a lactiferous menagerie my daughter's not

one with but closer & in mind maybe one
as in prayer or in throating this, cupful, cold,

or yesterday's earlier this a.m. You know
everything's repetitive & nothing repeats,

as in whoever said Sally Barger's father Roy
had his ashes cooked into rubber for a wheelbarrow,

its punctureless tire, when the cancer finally
got him. As in storms skinnydipping over

Purgatory & on over Cove & Apple Orchard,
Pine Ridge & Bryant Ridge, dusk's fabric a fierce

in sheets & streaks, tearing. There that slug
near the rainbarrel's sternum, ducks doing some

stutterstuff in puddle at flank of leafmulch
and hurricane fence. Blackberries big as,

toad in Swiss chard's rainbow room, creekstone
along the path, border as path. Moths at floods,

spiders busy with munch, processing & repair –
we watch them nights, their sticky doilies,

gossamer gondolas, & don't at all feel all
the identities one might identify & enteat, how

katydids, meantime, rewind night's cassette,
and the dry spot on the elm's trunk after

the latest stormpour is a long-armed lady
seen from behind holding on tight. Look,

Polly's nearly empty. She's trying to kick.
Udder to bucket, Sophie keeps at it. I grip

between hock & dewclaw, a hammerhandle
but hairier. Godly, good, a house of ducts

branching: milk-secreting alveoli,
progesterone the spark at first & then

inhibitor – corpus luteum: here comes
prolactin, some sucking stimulus. Are

you thirsty? I'm thirsty. Because who's playing
the organ playing the organ that makes

this miracle bodily mindful so Kirsten
can keep making what the twins need &

get, bloodtaxis ushering milkstuff to cells,
microhotels, five hundred parts blood to

one part milk – lipogenesis, energy as
synthesis, glucose & galactose

spawning lactose, milksugar, but only
in bits, milk ninety percent water,

nearly. I mean, yesterday at the creek
a sandpiper scribbled not an inch above

Sophie's back en route to land on ledge
a few feet downstream of where girl still

floated, bellydown, goggles on, staring at
light through water through current on rocks

and fish. Shadow & shine, time is, & summer
is, as milk, time, sweet & fat as a fencepost

for years hosting the same honeysuckle vine;
a feathered thing, too: mockingbird in blackberry,

swallows & thrush & jays. Catbird. Junco.
Crow, vulture, cardinal, wren. Get this:

Angie & Patricia for my birthday in May
hand over a cooler, say open it. Inside

a baggie loaded with slick burgundy bulges –
forty chicken hearts one day removed

from the birds they'd worked for, been.
Cornish cross, hefty meat birds lovelyladies

raise pastured in hoophouses. Size of plums
bumped from tree when mowing in late May;

yep, plum full of hearts the skillet soon was,
plus red wine, tamari, maple syrup,

black pepper, salt. I love hearts, how they sort
of bounce around your mouth when you bite –

no joke, summer's essence is density;
around here anyway, summer in these hills,

so much generous with green & growth.
Humid days the air seems to milk us, breathe

us; grass grows around our waists & chests,
up our legs. Dogs bark less. And then a coldfront

might roll in like mercy for a day or two, plow
the moisture out – you can tell the different trees

in the monster armchair of cove & ridge a mile across
the James then – oak, hickory, maple, gum.

Goat kids hop more often then. Bleat less, both
kind of kids. Crisper colors. Birds at amplitude

of lively & feeding. Chiggers, ticks. Bumblebees
in sunflower's pupil. Fig tree's fists starting

to close against cinderblock shed's southfacing.
Feels like September then. Feels like, like

the choreswarm is plenty, which it is, more
than plenty – mist some mornings coming up-

hollow from river: gravel & grass: there,
chainlink fencestapled to the six panel,

visibility a hundred yards, three bantam
roosters still shrillsounding – by that we

navigate, & by else: moss on lumber,
lichen on stone. Wormfossils, maybe,

in quartzite, preserved burrows (skolithus
tubes), shafts of other realms, other coolings,

later or sooner. God's calcium. Hoofprints.
Petrified beach. The prehistoric present, wants

unhinged, when what is resourceful to one
is handout to another. Even the fog rains.

Every thunderstorm lays an egg. Nothing new.
The next rooster starts before the first

finishes. Such is song. And milk. And milking –
or of. By the needful, the undoing that does it

done, we chug along: Kirsten, Sophie,
William, Ola, animals, soil, greens. The cool

doesn't last but she remembers it, Sophie
does, in triple digits (hottest July on record)

already at seven a.m. while drawing brush
over flank of the next-to-be-milked, giving

Geraldine a little sweet talk, watching
stray hairs drop on gravel & then wiping

her teats clean & stripping first squirts
from each to little dish for kitty to lick –

sweat on forehead, shirtwet. Days so hot you
breathe wool. Breathe what you can. Body adjusts.

Leaves shrivel. Petals do wilt. We slice tomatoes,
snip basil, monge bricks of chevre fresh or

frozen. In sunflower's radar. And freeze berries.
Picked, bagged with a vacuum sealer. There's haze.

Breezes in locust, breezes dancing with
each leafy thing. How into this world the babies

grow. Accustomed, maybe. Will they remember
any of it? – that question is one source,

leopardslug size of a mouse another, & always
more half gallon Masons blurring the life

seen through. Bleat on, kids. Hornet on hose nozzle.
Ridge on ridge. I'm saying, Geraldine hauls

a mighty shapely udder, teats just right for
Sophie's hands (a bit small for mine). No more

east or west, just the place, homestuff. Sip it,
white's original pale. And these handpainted signs

hacked from trash-lumber pile when whoever
remodeled the old bait shop on Purgatory Creek

into a rental house dumped it there. *Lizards.*
Hellgrammites. Red on white. Vertical.

Faded, chipped. Scraped & sanded & varnished
one Saturday afternoon next to the milking stand

and Pack n Play, in building you don't call
a building – more a frame, a sunshade. Port, too.

But name that summer. Name it: Kicky doe.
Sleepless. Chiggerlove. Babies. Goats. Chickens.

Eggs & milk. Stuff. Stuff & Grub. To build
a milking stand you need to procrastinate –

funny how that word works your mouth –
you don't have to have substantial scrap,

semi-substantial: six to fifteen foot of 1x6 stock
(old fascia works well), two lengths at least

six foot a piece for front feet & flyway, place
you catch goat by neck by space & feed,

hunger & blunt cunning, & hold her so
you can sit comfortably & work her udder dry;

i.e. steal her milk, accept the gift by doing
the work – work that hot dark bag as Sophie

now, two hands, each curling down, index
to pinkie, always down, down to streak canal,

two teats, wrist twisting, too – full teat, filling
teat – top to bottom like a pastry bag;

and you need a pad & a frame for that pad
and for the rear legs & flyway legs. Serious

jackleg carpentry, older school the better
but sure there's a place for flourishes, paint,

details jigsawed along some edge. Sturdy's
the goal; they appreciate it – Polly,

Geraldine, Matilda, Nellie – in that order
this morning, & each – back in June

we took a few hours one afternoon to
build this second milking stand. Even had

linoleum leftover from that cut
the Wilsons gave us for the first. Scrap is

scrappy – what's there what is, make it work,
hold you in its waters under cliffs where

moss tooths crevices & lichen makes continents
and archipelagos on the face, hold you down

at the base of a little falls, eyes & nose just
above surface, a loud so quiet a shape

might form, links piece together this way
and that way & another several, the way you

might climb from that water onto a boulder
and lie on your back looking at trees & sky &

water giving light to the underbelly
of some overhang in shapes of pulse,

current, & there know less of everything:
how summer is drip & seep: fireweed,

Joe Pye. Polypody. Names. Cracks of, of
abundance, the rush, the republic

of green, of flood. Thick stillnesses. Birdnoise,
bugnoise. Heat more than warmth, humidity

more than any, othermore. And sultrier. As
clover, sunflower puckering. Two by stock,

okay. Six on the width or eight, okay,
is needed so as to cut the transept-like

opening for doe's head, & two or oneplus
is plenty width for depth needed to sink

the pin that holds the guillotinish PVC
over neck keeping doe stanchioned to eat

from bucket wedged in cantilevered
feeddeck. There. And there. Wood. A tear out,

remnants of linen closet where we stood
the fridge when we moved a dishwasher

in the kitchen, nice doug fir two by four,
pry old nails out. And decking from shelves,

wide stuff, polycoated. Okay, some extra
spiral-shanked siders to fasten it. Skilsaw,

level, tape, pencil, razor knife – power
to extension, sawhorses & – presto – & –

snap – & – mark – & – blade – & – dust.
Speedsquare, jimmy it this, & this, &

tap, tap, & smack, sink that hot-dipped galvie –
we had the flyway together, rough cut oak,

old fenceboards from Solitude Farm, gift
from Sidney Thompson who manages

the place. Babies were sick then. Ola first,
paled & puked. Glands swelled. Fussed a bit

but mostly cheerful despite the gunk.
We feared tick-born, had removed a few

from each by then, little & big ticks –
behind the ear, in folds of leg, hips, neck.

I strolled them most mornings that spring
into pasture to do poultry chores &

refresh water for sheep & barn cats &
guardian dogs. If then, the ticks, or off

of us – who knows. Good thing Doc said nothing
to do with ticks. A virus. Wait it out.

Give care. Ola recovered, then William
dazed, pale, wailing, puking. We cared, milked,

ate, swum, visited. Spring's burst,
summer's creep. We sung stilling blends –

lullaby & nonsense rhyme, jigs & ditties
by riverful. Soon we were banging

the rear legs of stand to flyway by ledger
and joist, four long by two foot wide. Bracing

triangles at corners (more old shelving cuts)
to fasten decking to legs, linoleum stapled

to decking for cleaning-ease, vinegar
and wipe after each milking. Red oak,

old boards, the flyway – thirty two inches
to transept-base (from decking not ground),

and nine-plus from feed bucket perch to that point,
transept about nine inches diameter, enough

of a hole for Nubian's ears, pendulous
and vein-ridged elegances, all dangle & fine hair,

curl & flop & lovely strangenesses. Rain
the prior evening & now, almost

midday, mist just breaking, a breeze out
of the north, cool in shade where measured

and measured & measured again, & then cut
and fastened. Flies & moths, all manner of.

Cricket, bee. Other traffic. Bantam rooster
in cucumber's shade. Tomatoes reddening.

Egyptian walking onion like some forgotten
punctuation. Okra, lamb sounding for ewe.

Shadow & shine, everywhere, of invisibles –
microflora, nocturnals. And the promise

of milk. William's fever, broken, sired
a rash, pink & puffy, on cheek, nose, around

his eye. Talk about irritable. Sweet,
heartbreaking screeches & yowls. Sores

on his mouth, trouble nursing. Kirsten
tense with it, continents from decent sleep.

We talked, hugged, little resolved save
some stubborn resolve hardening – call it

marriage, parenthood, life, or gravity,
inertia, eighteen years together now –

we visited my mother one long weekend,
where with other siblings visiting there

were three kids under one & one two
year old, so babble, baby toys, little sleep,

good laughter, chat, meals. Was a fine visit
but we ran out of the milk we brought –

Polly, Geraldine, Matilda, Nellie –
by lunch on the second day, & I felt

emptier then, less sturdy, steady even
while thinking of our pal Tommy swinging by

our place morning & evening to care
for animals, feed & water, fetch eggs

and so on. He didn't milk. The kids took care
of that, goat kids, we left them on,

as they say, instead of locking them in
pigpen each evening for twelve hours off,

time for udders to refill, be again
like a big dark fruit we'd juice the pulp of,

though with more reverence than that. See,
you have to be clean about it all –

there is much care given to that, to
clean milk. A clean stand is crucial, & once

the doe is on the stand, locked in with
a bit of feed in bucket on perch, you brush

her coat real well & talk soothing or sing
to clean her of any worry, let the letdown begin,

loosen that sphincter. In '56, Mackenzie
in *Goat Husbandry* wrote, "Even if we put

the goat on some form of insulated
and impervious floor, her dung pellets hop

about like a packet of spilled peas here,
there, and everywhere under her feet

to be trampled to dust and onto her bed
to contaminate her coat." No dung dust.

You brush. Flank & neck, hips, belly, even
the udder & tail, triangular flap

I glance at again, rearview, on Geraldine
while kneeling here, keeping her legs down,

steady, with firm & gentle grip, & letting
the motions of it – Sophie's work, the babies,

life on the edges – milk other motions.
And then with a different brush, give the stand

another once over or twice. Goats like being
brushed. Some days less so & like less then

when you take the wipe to the teats & bag
and clean that real well before squeezing those

first squirts into container that goes under
the stand for cats & corgi to lop. Now

a fresh wipe to clean your hands or have
on hand in case you have to grab anything

before udder's slack. Like from Pack n Play
a baby who might be maxed out or sitting,

kicking or rolling or fondling some toy or
bodypart, label or dustbunny, maybe

both babies. Mercy, yes, a fine breeze has
kicked up now as Sophie strips last squirts,

taut yarn, from Geraldine. Bumblebees forage
on Echinacea pistils. Crows fuss in far pines.

Purgatory looms, three cell towers vague
in the haze. Beau, the male Pyrenees –

Stella's stud – barks & chases a Harley, no,
a farting hell of Harleys down on Arcadia Road.

The breeze takes babyswings in the maple
for a ride. Nellie stops at the trough, old

enamel tub, her long ears, longer even
than her snout, dipping in the water as

she sips, reminder of cold days in winter
when ice forms on their eartips. But when

was there ever a winter, I have to wonder
today, the way summer does smother – so

present, so in the place – much remembrance
or evidence of other seasons. See,

Geraldine's our kickiest doe, stamps
with poignant accuracy one cloven in

exact place your hand's working teat as if
to extract it, as if it hurts, but it's not about

that kind of hurt, I don't guess, but about
play & hunger. Her feed's low, she kicks. Eats

faster each time. Is she racing us? No, she wants
more. Maybe she's nervous. Sophie's good at

sensing the oncoming hoof, feels the slight shift
from bow to aft, weight to leg doe won't lift,

and often there's a shudder or flex in her flank
and neck, even a snort – so our girl might let go

one teat & hold bucket with that hand while
working the other, ready to slide the stainless

of fresh warm foamy out of the way of
dung-dusty hoof, shin, knee. One heatwave,

but they called it a heatdome for it gripped
the country like some gargantuan claw,

I was milking alone, & the does were
being superkicky (never a milking season

like this one for kicks), so I rigged a hobble
at stand's hind, carabinered a rope from

oak's base to a looped-cinch system, webbing
around doe's shin. Some kicked less (Nellie &

Geraldine) while others kicked more with
kicking made sloppy & painful-seeming

by tangle. Captivity: the goat life, the milk life,
part of the deal, you know, something to

wonder, try to remedy, a curiosity, part
of the spill, division of meal, spell

of harvest – squirt & squeeze, a ritual we do
and undo, drink from, did & will. One morning

late July, I sat in mist at maple, Feisty in swing,
grunting & cooing, brother Mellow still down

for first nap. Was a breeze, damp & cool.
Were six chicks in hoophouse adjacent,

and they sounded like standing under
a massive powerline on scrubby ridgeflank,

enough kilowatts in air to power
some devious device. Ola hummed, hymned,

I drank a cup of milk. Seventeen spiderwebs
as if various explanations of beauty

and chaos, & symmetry, & the chaos
in beauty & wonder of how one thing

gets a meal, a little & pretty creepy thing
out of work & magic, bodywork &

bodymagic (you won't see Kokopelli in
these ampersands). I drank the milk & mist

and pasture in the milk & laughed with Ola,
swinging her & swinging me, & drank milk

from the sunlight coming through the maple
and through & off the mist the spiderwebs

and fields held, & watched the does in gulch,
the northwest corner, making milk, letting

the kids take it, or walking on like some
dolphin-manatee cross in a green bay

tidal with stickweed, breezes, shadow,
various infinities seething or else just

getting by, & it tasted good, sweet &
cold, a distillation of ground, this ground

and the grounding motions of all involved,
the family of families I've got to keep

throwing hay to. Belly tickled with each sip.
Say sweet, say precious – you want some filtered

and cold? Here, stand in this jigsaw of light
& shadow splashed under the maple. Hear

the diva Ola tell of whatever she tells
as William (now awake) bops her with spatula

and smiles & coos, despots of the Pack n Play.
For the ritual we do it & how out

of the ritual – of place, doing – comes the taste,
and soon the place, each part, micro & macro,

teensy & monstrous, is milk & drink looped,
lopped, tasted – culture it, you got landscape

got yogurt, got cheese. Or homescape, garlic
scape pesto thickened with chevre. Pour off

the whey for dogs, chickens, ducks. Milk enough
reading & a poem might be dragging

a cricket mulchwise, some hungry wasp, for
a meal under a cohosh leafroof. Or milk,

the milking, as manuscript, line after line,
collaborative – Sophie's hands, doe's teats –

milk as ink – milk-in-bucket as book,
stainless bound early draft soon to be

filtered – revised – into glass & cooled.
Later, you read a sip or culture a pot

at proper temp – collage it, a remix &
regrowth, bacterial choreography or

gardening. Can't forget Byron, stinky &
handsome buck, who bred these does, helped make

the kids to make milk flow, how Sophie assisted
does delivering kids in spring. We milk

our babies to sleep, six sessions, two babies,
two naps & bedtime each day, Kirsten giving

breastly goodness before we each work
one baby's udder empty of awake

with quiet motions, rocking & song. Hell
yes they scream. Really howl, in stereo,

the anti-lullaby. *But it's a cool night in July,*
clouds still bright, the sun bye bye. Soon

the moon is gonna rise, we'll go walking
down the gravel drive. Chickens on the roost,

there goes a goose. Dogs are fed, hogs gone
to bed. Hear the whippoorwill in the bottomland,

just a little while I'm gonna take your hand
and walk on down the gravel drive, side by side,

just you & I. And so on, steady-voice, hand
rubbing babe's back, fingertickling neck. *Clouds*

like salmon & the crickets are a jamming,
clouds so pink you just gotta wink. Corny,

sure – cornier the better. Slow breathing voice,
a calm, soulful voice. *Goats in the barnyard*

chewing their cud – we're still learning the ways
of love. Baby, I'll be a lightning bug

in your wicker chair, just pass me a jug
of that good corn liquor there. Yea, I'll be

the crocodile in your evening wear,
I'll be the smile on your dancing bear,

be anything you wanna dare, just pass
me a jug of that fresh goat nectar there.

Sophie stands, bucket of Geraldine in hand,
doe finishing what feed's still in bucket.

Daughter Sophie, big sister Sophie. This work
but one love of hers, & the love in her doing

of the thing, if lucky, in this making,
this singing. Gob of salve in hand, I wipe

Geraldine's udder, stretch a bit, & then,
while Sophie sisters her back to pasture

and to fetch Matilda, I carry the pail
to kitchen, strain & filter & get

the goods in sterile Mason submerged
to just under the lid in ice water, as in

a portrait made one day two years ago,
not long after Clementine kidded out

Geraldine:

CROWDED BARNYARD, PRETTY SPRING DAY, ONE LITTLE GOAT

now sprawls against the fence. Now bends a foreleg under.
           Now gums a stalk, tongue so pink
      the fescue seems to bleed. Look,

her head is anvil. Her ears, ridged by veins, flop & curl. Curl
           & quiver. I like them. Streaks
      of dark, streaks of pale. Elegant frames

for an elegant neck. I like the way the long ears of these
           Nubians splay the ground – outriggers,
      landing gear – a full inch before the lips

part, dark lips, revealing the kernels of her tiny, ancient teeth.
           This is graze. This is abdomen,
      the fast throb. Lava tubes of her pupils:

what they see is what they see. But now her legs, four Floridas,
           erotic with flex, send her flying
      to perch on the overturned enamel tub,

a 180 mid-air, some little skate rat. It's hard to keep up.
           I'm breaking in pieces. Of giggle.
      Perfect. And the fence is a dulcimer, too.

Posts for frets. Wire for strings. Play it, little goat. Let the breeze.
           Let the sun, shadow machine.
      Showy, showy & a bit spastic, her hop

from tub. Dainty, cloven toes. Now Mama's here, Miss Clementine,
        so doeling kneels, tail atwitch,
    neck jive-pistoning for milk

to run. But not for long. Mama needs shade. So doeling prances.
        And then she bounds. A walnut
    burning. A nimble, hazardous balance.

A hormone's a gobblygloo that's produced
by one organ or gland but has a zizzle

on a different, often remote organ – so
when Sophie's singing, as she is now

to Matilda (my favorite doe), this juices
nerves in her brain, & other nerves now jump

as Sophie brushes her & wipes her teats,
singing all the while: *Cluck old hen, cluck*

old hen, ain't laid an egg since way back when –
fun song she saws on fiddle. Stimulation

in loops: udder & ear & girth & flank
to brain & back from pituitary's two lobes

along Artery Road. That day we built
the second milking stand we cut two more

triangles on which to hang the feed deck
off the uprights, five sheetrock screws on

the vertical, two above to hold the scrap
sheathing, which once fastened did meet the blade

of a heavy jigsaw working the circle
the width of bucket under its lip. Not

fussy work but quick, satisfying as
any made, useful thing, especially

from what once was – remade, repurposed –
with rough simplicity of use, sixteen cuts,

six triangles, the rest rectangular;
muttishly made, for sure, & soon to be

varnished with oils of goat, milk, & saliva
from snorts & coughs. Fine breeze now, but the sun

digs its claws in harder, too. Pack n Play
in shade. Ola smiling. William deep in wonders

of some shard of leaf he's fingering. Soon
they'll nap. The day will heat more. We'll look west

in hopes of rainclouds, a storm. We need rain.
We always need rain in August, & if

the need is code for other things, reliefs
as soothing as rain but more to do with soul

than soil or level in the well or rainbarrels,
o well. I remember the fire, the heat

of those crazy March hours we were driving –
it was cold – back from North Carolina,

my brother-in-law's wedding, & had stopped
to pick up some goats that friends of friends

were giving away, purebred Alpines,
the mama in milk. This was Warren County,

east & north of Raleigh where piedmont meets
the coastal plain in scrappy but pleasant,

rolling pineland. Our first goats, these were,
six years ago. We'd loaded mama goat

in truck's bed under a cap with two
three month old kids & a couple squarebales,

Kirsten next to me in cab, Sophie – then
eight – next to her entranced & delighted as

seven day old buckling lapward sucked
her finger as if teat. The slant six

in Lillie Mae, our old Dodge pickup,
was thirsty too, so we stopped for gas

outside South Boston, former tobacco town
in Southside VA. Kirsten & Sophie took

the kid to play in a grassy place adjacent;
I had to use restroom so left pump running

and ran inside one of those minimarts
where the light is like an X-ray & things

scream buy me in a way so disgustingly
seductive your soul could be a made

for TV special with eight million viewers,
prime time! – soon returned to truck & goats,

peered under the fiberglass cap Tommy
had salvaged from somebody's junk. Smoke,

a thin plume, rose from one of the bales.
I lifted the rear window, moved the bale;

twine broken, it opened, a sort of bellows.
Flames leapt. More flames. Day skipped

to a harder song. In an hour, a bad,
fateful hour made tender by help of strangers,

we were waiting for the vet, standing in grass,
truck soaked & black, cap melted, glass smudgy

and curled or else in shards. Sophie held buckling,
offered her finger, which it took greedily.

I watched the wind. I don't know what I watched.
"Daddy," she said. "When you were little, did

you see anything burn?" "A house," I said
after a pause. "But nobody was in it."

How memory's udder fills up & shrinks
no matter how many of the mind's hands

grasp those ten thousand teats. Life is milk,
milks us too. And is more, way more: clouds

in curds on sky's blue porcelain, bright of
fig leaf's underbelly, cedars yellowing,

blackberries, tithonia, all this but a drop
in the milking bucket of time & being,

unbeing. And then Sophie held the drill,
three eighths bit, & turned an opening for

the eyebolt to hold the PVC stanchion
in place above doe's neck while eating

and standing still enough for one to drain
her udder – turned an opening in

so much not yet & already open,
seed to stem to leaf to fruit & then

to seed again – this summer, too, this day –
the milk to yogurt to whey to chevre;

the bamboo baby spoon to lip to cheek
to diaper to smile & scream, & yes

we worried how large William's head
at the next well-baby, off the charts;

and smiled at his cute & peaceful ways next
to sister Ola, rapt & attentive & engaged,

nearly a showoff, talking even now to
Matilda from Pack n Play as Sophie

kneads one teat, next teat, white stream spraying
a bit, & I kneel at rear, hand-shackling legs

(I like the view); talks this potbelly babygirl,
hand & mouth, turning wrists & fingers like

a drill, fitting wonder a place for another
fastening. I think of the lime green spraybottle

Sophie uses to hold back the does who
won't wait their turn to be milked

but crowd the gate, pushy & strong,
wanting fed, brushed, relieved of udder-weight

probably too – I don't know what goats want
but they sure love these brown larvae-like tubes –

steam crimped oats, steam flaked corn,
coarse cracked corn, wheat middlings, dehulled

soybean meal, corn distillers, dried grains,
cane molasses & so on – plenty of vitamins,

supplemental copper, too. Crude protein
eighteen percent. Numbers, factoids, dimensions,

volume. Something holy in the use & making,
the composition of it all, akin to accuracy

not just technicalspeak but a way
to a common language, to health &

regularity. And mystery. Blue Seal
Coarse Goat Feed – I like knowing

their offices are in Londonberry, NH,
gives the milk something solid, placed,

even if only a quarter Folger's can
mornings to keep them calm & held, bulk

of nourishment from field & brush. Summer,
summer, summer – less like merry go round

than paw paw tree bearing weight
of vine – greenbriar, fox grape. See the old

bedding hay in crush & run, hen feathers
tattered & dusty from molt in stray

depressions where in more rainy times
puddles the rainbarrel-overflow. See, roseola

cleared in William & Ola Rose,
and we had a few days of good health

before some new gunk began, Ola first:
high fever, upchuck, then diarrhea for

a week, William the same with a few days
lag. Care, animal care. Food & fluid &

love & fevers. Up & Up Size Three diapers.
Good gracious. Kirsten had it next, probably

best for her to stay in bed, sleep all day,
day William still hurt with fever, bellytoil,

squirtpoops, a Saturday, humid as crotchtree,
that joint where dark & absence of dark,

childhood & maturity, yessir & no ma'am –
and I had already drunk, no, savored

two metal cups of goat milk to chase
the coffee & fortify gut, shoulders, soul

for holding babies when Sophie came in
the kitchen in tears to say Bessie's dying –

Bessie our first ewe, then seven, having
dropped twelve lambs in six years – strong,

delightfully grumpy ewe that by three
that afternoon after four hours with mattock

and shovel & a bag of lime rested four feet
under a place in the pasture where in

winter we finish our sled runs, a church
of pastureground at bottom, not far off

the catalpa that was sending big palmates
down the way happens that pre-fall

of late summer – old Bessie, may she rest
at all now relieved of that constant grazing,

hunger, duty – how many lambs you did
suckle, & of them, the males we've so enjoyed

the legs of, shanks & loin chops, ribs –
luckily Suzi Branch came around eleven,

helped with babies – too hot & macabre to
roll them down in babyjogger, park

under catalpa or set up Pack n Play while
cutting in drydirt a place for Bessie. You

could say we were fertilizing the field,
Bessie & us, but let's not go there nor

back to organic feed for the does,
though they deserve it – feedcosts are crazy

enough: fifteen bucks a fifty pound,
organic twenty five plus a longer drive,

though I miss the way that feed screamed
to be boiled in a pot with butter & salt

for a tasty lunch: Countryside Organics
out of Waynesboro, mixing up goodstuff,

organic field peas, organic barley,
organic oats, organic alfalfa meal,

organic wheat, organic flaxseed,
organic rice bran, organic corn,

sodium silico aluminate, dried
organic kelp, organic coconut oil,

sea shell flour, dried lactobacillus
acidophilus, & more. Morgan drove

over that day to help bury Bessie –
so kind of him, real friend. I'd work

the mattock, he'd shovel the softened earth
from pit, throw in heaps growing. We talked,

looked. Deer season felt closer than it was,
Bessie on her side starting to ripen,

and Suzi, sweet, funny Suzi, in swing
with Ola on the hill a hundred yards

off, Kirsten napping with William, Sophie
playing fiddle, cutting up some old tunes:

Bonaparte's Retreat, *Whiskey Before Breakfast*,
and that Irish jig, *Pull the Knife & Stick it*

Again. Now Nellie walked up on Morgan
and me, & who knows what she knew only

it was more than I'd ever, & maybe she
was missing Clementine, doe we'd sold

that week to Mrs. Whitley who farms near
the jail in Troutville – see, Nellie & Clem

were the alpha does, & I have a hunch,
or maybe I'm projecting, that Nellie

didn't want to be in charge on her own
or didn't quite trust Mrs. Whitley, though

Sophie & Ki sensed she was a fine goatherd
first time she came out & walked Clementine

to the stand without fuss & stood by
as the doe hopped up, not a lick of feed

in bucket on deck to cajole her, & stood
still while Mrs. Whitley felt her udder,

her asymmetrical teats, & liked her anyway
or because of that. Goat people can be

as fussy as their animals with selectivity
and culling for production & so forth.

I miss Clementine. She was chilling
and her nose had this awkward bridge

that distinguished her from the others –
even her kids – & allowed for a bit of

goofiness into the nobility
of that Roman nose that along with

the long, dangling ears have the breed,
Nubian, written all over. Paper,

I kid you not, is milk. And milk a kind
of paper the body writes its stories

of energy on. Nothing crazy about it,
nothing but a dense white liquid

that soothes & calms & nourishes &
is fun to procure. "Lois comes today,"

Sophie says, her two braids snaking ears
to shoulders. Girl's down to the last strips.

Matilda's finished her feed. She waits,
kicks not. "I wonder what she'll bring this time,"

Stronghands says from around the flank, as
from around these late mornings once a week

when, chores done, one baby or both down,
we're munching a late breakfast or dealing

with some phone calls or still cleaning up,
here comes beautiful Lois Bisese to fetch

some goods from us & drop off a loaf
or two from the bakers at Breadcraft

(who use her hens' eggs) & visit a bit –
farmtalk, kidtalk, familytalk – all of us

swimming in day's milk, cloudmilk, milking
one another for nourishment, stays

against loneliness, misinformation, &
whatnot – spooky how the other morning

we found a mess in the feed room at barn,
storage cans, big ones, overturned, chest

of medical supplies, fifty pounds
or so, moved a few feet, opened, & gear

scattered all over with no evidence
or clear sense as to who or what

might have made such a ruckus out there
against the foliage-dense thickets of briar,

vine, paw paw, oak that inhabits the sinkhole
against which the barn's rear (farthest

from house) sits weathered & silent not as
if immune to each year's growth but resigned,

confident plenty in its footers, post-depths –
settled, in other words, in its settling.

Wondered bear, wondered human. Weird
to see so little feed eaten. No clawmarks,

no scat, nothing stolen or damaged just
that strange grace: visitation. Yep, goats

were freaked, wouldn't enter the room where
normally they crowd at gate, mob-like

with flood's surge & strength. Caleb the corgi
zipped frenetic to various corners –

barked alarming, & at the space behind
the salvaged chest freezer we use to store

bags of feed, he dug & whined & scratched
tweaky-vibed as all get out. I poked around

with the old twelve gauge & next night set Beau
the stud great Pyrenees, square-headed &

ram-shouldered, out there to guard the place.
Who knows what he heard smelled saw but

nothing out of place in morning or next few
he patrolled the nights of. How this summer

is not this summer but all the summers,
all predators over years caught, uncaught

trespassing or not. Crush & run under boot.
Clang & swivel & hiss of bucket,

stainless, & handle. Brush against flank.
Udder heat, limbs in wind. Or rain on leaf

off another leaf, drop. Feed buckets by
handle hung on hooks according to order   .

of procession – Polly, Geraldine, Matilda,
Nellie – four plastics that once held

real yummy coconut oil. Hoof-trimming snips
on nail next nail up, broom in corner,

trash bucket, metal trashcans for feed &
minerals, some dog or other in shadows,

dusty barncat invisible yet watching
always, way spiders in rafters watch

whatever they watch with – silk maybe,
though much else besides. My jigsaw cut

was nicht gut – the feedbucket didn't fit,
so we corrected that, tried Sophie's hands

in stand's making but not quite big enough
to work powertools safely. She sunk nails,

sunk a few screws too with eighteen volt
cordless Porter Cable. William sure likes

that drill, positively writhes at sight of it
& sound, that whine & turning. Some days

this summer I strap him on chest by hijinks
of webbing foam cordura buckles, or

strap Ola on – whoever isn't napping or seems
most ripe for jaunt, & we head off to see

the goats making milk, browsing orchard &
quackgrass, summer's early leaf-fall, too –

catalpa, sycamore, locust, oak. Ola claps
and coos & grunts to see them seeing her

quick moment before more munch – boughs,
their needle-dainty nibbles of cedar

and scrub pine, or tearing fingernail-sized
foliage of briar & other shrubs, vines.

William stares, mostly quiet, & kicks.
Tremors sometimes. Goats never stay one place

for long as if anxious for some new taste
or nourishment, instinct guiding them –

and grace, the right mineral, protein – away
from poison. They do like poison ivy,

are hardly bothered by thorns & spines.
Twins – & me too – like best when having

browsed to a certain height a tree or shrub,
they stand on hind legs – head back, neck

stretched – and reach, forelegs resting on trunk
or another goat's flank, to tear leaves & other

roughage from elevations the owls might prey
from at night. How their udders dangle then,

teats jiggling – evidence of divinity in difference
between product & source – milk as foreign

in appearance to those dark hot wrinklies
as hoping to write a poem that powers off

every single computer in the world
for a while & for good is to prayer, simple

as God, give us the milk, the words – o yes,
Thy will, not mind, be done. Or milking stand

to saw & drill of its origins. Rare mornings
you pour from bucket to filter tray

exact amount needed to fill Mason jar
not one drop over or under half gallon,

slide tray to other jar & get it right
again or not. Usually not this summer

of Polly, Geraldine, Matilda, Nellie,
milk like, what? – not godsemen, goddess

letdown – who knows but stuff's so tasty
it must be holy, must be made by careful

and caring husbandry & wifery, research,
hardware, nutrients, instincts, meaning

heart, a kind of milk-yearning heartherding,
many little labors & connections like day

Gerald Breedon helped load fifty bales,
the good hay he makes – orchard grass &

timothy cut early enough & baled dry
and green – helped by throwing those lunkers,

fifty pounders, up on the old Dodge where
I stacked & stole glances around his land

there above Middle Creek, high ground,
several hollows beginning at & between

the compass points, a good, big garden,
root cellar, equipment, sheds, even the old

carbide setup by apple orchard on
southfacing edge. We sat on the porch

after last load & chatted. I baited him
about places & things, who & what & when,

and Gerald, having been born here as
his father & father's father, was eager

to fill me in, being Thursday & him not
working till weekend swing at cement plant

in Catawba. He drank a cold beer,
which gave some cotton to his twang, &

grasshoppered from talk of poachers to
iron, pig iron & furnaces like the one down

the road near his homeplace on Jennings Creek;
and from there to the man, a Markham, who built

Gerald's house & used to go by horseback
to run the mill on Purgatory Creek

at Pattonsburg & back home again three
or four ridges & three or four times that

in mileage. "Guess what that window cost,"
Gerald said, busky mustache caterpillaring

as he spoke & pointed to wavy glass
over the front door. "Markham, see, kept

his receipts," Gerald said. "I've got them all."
"A buck & a half," I said. Or was it barter,

I wondered privately. "Thirty cents,"
Gerald said. Six turkey hens at field's edge,

doe & fawn north of there, cicadas turning
their rainsticks, though it was dry then,

burnban dry, oppressive, seed-making,
seed-dropping, leaf-turning dry. So summer cuts

its teeth. We had one hundred & ten bales
in barn after the last load, & somewhere

a goldfinch perched on sunflower's puckered,
black on forehead, black on wings, & withal

a yellow paler & as sweet as a memory trace
of Sophie, Kirsten, the twins gone to

Natural Bridge with the Nelson kids,
those pals of Sophie soon headed

to Maine to start another life among
a conservative Mennonite church community –

paint your vehicle black, straw hats & parts
down the middle for men, sacky, patternlesses

for women – no pleats, no fancy stuff – modest
and simple. Strange to think Sophie's friend,

the oldest, was done, being female & almost
fifteen, with school; no, more than strange –

complicated & freeing, &, yes, the kids do play
so well, gently & with little hogwash:

no celebrity mimicry, no TV
or computadora zombiestuff but

a reverence for small things, birds, plants,
bugs; as well a hands-on ethic, no problem

jumping in to help in kitchen or garden,
shed or field. Real pleasure & gratitude

in making, in process, in materials.
I was sad they were leaving, Rob & Judy

and the kids with their hardcore straightedge
Biblicality day in & day out & never

trying to push the stuff on us but willing
to help & be helped, generous with knowledge,

tools. Devotion. I was sad. I was baffled
by the fact I wouldn't be baffled by

the same species of bafflement as often
once they left, that you-all-are-intense-

&-I'm-not-cutting-such-mustard stuff,
that stuph with a ph instead of f,

twin f identical or not according
to handwriting. And humidity &

handwriting have much in common, don't
ask me what, what a summer, this last moon

after hearing Sophie play fiddle for
a couple of tunes with Wes Chappell

and No Strings Attached at Fincastle Winery,
full moon mostly cloudsmirched but beaming

in shafts now & then, cloudoscopically,
our Helpxhelper (see helpx.net),

Guillaume, an engineer from France, having
just arrived & at the cabin with his girlfriend

Rachel who drove them down from
Baltimore (great, gritty city, ever eaten

at Birds of a Feather?), full moon of the first
good rain in over a month, land so thirsty

it slurps your soul so you're so thirsty,
even thirstier, & go slurping some other,

smaller soul, setting a mouse trap perhaps
or not feeling up for carrying

another bucket of scraps to barn, so chickens
don't get a treat now. A baffling moon,

and many days this summer baffling, &
many bafflements baffling, & goat milk

always to unbaffle, lip to tongue
to throat to belly – simple but not &

pale but not unless deep pale – more nourishing
than white, & here's Nellie, & here's Sophie

rubbing her down & around with brush,
and twins a bit fussy but chilling enough

in Pack n Play soon enough to stand
against the sides of it, & fall, & Kirsten

in kitchen chugging kefir. Life in bucket
on stand in eye & hand. And what is more

womanly, more female than milk. Pale
like ash in grilling fire, whitewater in

moonlight. Is this, the origins of milk,
the femininity, why people fear it

raw, fear it even when procured in
clean & loving conditions, & filtered right

away, & then cooled, jarred, jar set in
cooler of ice water. Lack of sterility?

Pale fact of it? The thievery? The kid,
doe or buck, that goes without? Sandstone pale.

And the sound of the bleat: fathoms pale.
I have seen the milk's dream-self flying

around the pasture nights this summer,
riding what thermals from lightning bug

to lightning bug to bat to cicada's flashmob,
all the swells, screech owl spookadelic &

mournful downhollow below Crouch's place,
but the night after July's full moon

the milkghost, it drifted from doe to doe
where they lay under barn-eave, & it touched

their ears with some odd & flighty mojo
for soon there were six does soaring like hawks

in loops, banking heavy & sure around
the old, wizened catalpa in the bottom,

those long Nubian ears outstretched & longer,
it seemed, working like wings, legs tucked under,

tails up as if for steerage, feisty, caprine grin
on their tight-lipped muzzles – Polly, Geraldine,

Matilda, Nellie – & not always in that order
now but changing in & out of formation,

playing, yes, serious frolic, their grazing
and kidding needs on hold for a time.

I could have been a cloud. I wanted to try
to ride one, wanted to ride Nellie –

she seemed most daring & in control,
the alpha doe, & stoutest, a fine flyer,

but I ran inside to grab Kirsten & Sophie
and the twins for them to see & maybe

have a ride too. They looked at me, my wife
and oldest kid like the loony I still am, & then

saw – took a minute – that I was as serious
as an okra blossom & ran outside only

to find the does back under barn-eave
looking wan & disinterested. I shook

my head, shook from can to trough some feed
for does but they didn't want it – the ewes,

more bullish than sheepish, gulped it down,
baahing for more from get-go. "You need

a glass of milk," Kirsten said. "Sheep," I said.
"is to goat as" – & Sophie came in then,

said, "Paw paw is to fig." "Softcover is
to hardcover," I added. This went on:

cloud is to wind, pine is to oak, moor is
to scrub, sponge to brush, talk to thought,

music to painting. Nellie's trying to kick
again, her right leg mostly, but I'm holding

on. I'm flying, trailer she's hauling behind,
and Sophie's got those big teats in hands, &

I've got those sinewy legs in hands, & Nellie,
speed-eater, is kicking for more feed

in bucket, more grub. Sophie hooks her up,
wipes hands again & places bucket once

more under udder. Call it what you like –
yesterday Geraldine dunked hoof in

bucket. Everything was going so well.
She wasn't – or was she – looking after the dogs

and cats, for it was their milk now, hoofstamped
for them, & doggone right tails wagged, butts

jiggled, almost kept time with the crickets.
"The economic pros and cons are not

the decisive factor in goat-keeping,"
MacKenzie wrote. "… a matter of social value,

of the accepted way of life. Goat-keeping
is often a symbol of a deeply felt

minority faith. Between those who work
overtime in an uncongenial occupation

to buy labor-saving domestic gadgetry
and manufactured pleasures, and those

who cut the cost of living by the (to
them) congenial labor of goat-keeping,

gardening, and do-it-yourself, there is
a great gulf. From whichever side you view it,

Hell is on the other." Picture this:
an establishment, many of them, one

in each town of any size where in addition
to some tastoidal microbrew you have

on tap the local's best of that morning's
hand-drawn goat – won't say nectar again –

different fat content & tastes depending
on the lay of the land of the farm of

their origins, the (to be fancy & French
about it) *terroir* – how the soul of

a particular place gives each tap a flavor
distinct from the next, yogurts & kefirs

and soft cheeses, too, on the menu, no
big screen TV's channeling live feeds

from cameras mounted on various goats
of the herds & from various vantages –

barn, field, milking room, thicket, fencerow.
I don't know, but one thing I know for sure –

living without goats & without the milk
and breeding & birthing that begets it is

no longer an option. More than hobby,
more a full body, full day, full life need.

I look around Nellie's rump at Sophie
and see a girl so at home in her labors,

a girl glowing with love & gratitude
for these animals she cares for & care

for her, for all of us; & I see the X
the milk makes as she squeezes, instead

of one teat then next, both teats at once,
noise like a snare drum, hands opening

with simultaneous upward-udder bump
like the kids do with more force than seems

necessary, some bird – heron maybe –
beaking a meal. I see the X & in it

a little of this place, the hills & hollows,
before nine tenths of it all eroded over

eons to leave what's here as remnant
of what was & what will be, soil &

sediment; & for a time I'm with the changes,
the washing away, scour by refreeze by

melt by wind & old seas, tides, storms,
no calmer than that calm, that seeing more

feeling than seeing or even knowing,
time elongated & externally integrated

and pale like rocks in creekbed we explore
evenings in summer in swims & canoes

and just hanging around browsing on
sounds & smells – eddyflowers blossoming,

geese, green herons, blue heron, osprey,
eagle, vulture, crow. Kingfisher & mink

and muskrat & otter. Lots of deer, lots
of river rats, especially on weekends,

tubers & sit-on-top kayakers, some
fishing, many not fishing or fishing

less with monofilament than lines
the mind & body ride when adrift

on gradient, time's pulse, all the changes
defined by rain & other weathers. God,

I love to watch the pretty goats go by
in a line on their way to some green place

these late summer mornings, milking finished,
& there's Kirsten in nursing-flapped nightie,

sweet trawler between islands of perennials,
veggies, cutting, weeding, clouds a contortion

of upper & lower – marblelized – far
fingers of Hurricane Irene, baby

hanging on chest, other baby asleep,
diaper rash or tickbite to fret over,

dogs sacked out after long night barking
predators away, friends on their way,

hopes & fears here & more on the way,
replacement or offspring, grass needing

mowed, needing rain, many beds mulched
and covercropped with clover & hairy vetch,

layer of old hay like a runner rug
spindly & unfastened, heaviness behind

the eyes, Dodge needing an oil change, care
for the care. Yes, milk's tidal in its way –

pasture, udders, breeding & birth. Milk, days,
these doings thereout & in, flood & ebb

of blossom & stalk – this daze, time, bodies,
amplitudes & energies, butterflies &

bumblebees, basil & peaches. How on
that second milking stand we made, Sophie

stood to test stability & bearing capacity,
vibe of being up there, walked from end

to end, those ragamuffin salvaged boards
now in jackleg formation joined; how there,

already, on oak, left of the uprights, a moth,
and as soon as we see it: flying. How,

udder empty, Nellie stares over her shoulder
now, look on her face that stuns & shines

with what can't be known but surmised,
cared for, read. Globules, an effervescence –

how the foam has gathered near milkpail's rim,
crinkles of air releasing, let go. Yum.

DIRT

August now, & the okra are small trees,
barked at base & sumac-like

in their forking. Shade-dropped,
the lower branches – their scars stare,

cyclopic, into their own woody lids.
Simply by squatting, she's well hidden,

the woman, infant on her back (cloth-
wrapped) among the dozen plants

plugged into mulchswell. Serrated
and notched, the leaves have thickened,

each gummy-haired lobe, with age,
the age-old exchanges – matter, energy:

air, water, rock. She could stitch them –
as tough as rhubarb leaves

but not as smooth, as rich as a fig's,
though not as sharkskinned nor

as brittle – sew them with some
harvested twine into a blind to mask

her scent & possibly to lure a rare thing
into vision. See, on one green knuckle,

the yellowjacket, sluggish & sunlit,
stunned in its labor. Woman – they call

her Kirsten, Mama, Ki – she's more beautiful
to me, & dangerous, & nourishing, than

lightning, water, even death. She knows that
it's too late in the history of the world

to apologize for being amazed. Some leaves
rust – rust, too, is a kind of burning.

Flowers & fruit reach; dang, they aspire,
transpire – multibudded at peak, torch

as much as resting place; they look out,
they shine, the blossoms, their ivory,

pale butter, veined in bloodpink
that radiates from base, from source –

rootwork, seedspark – that forked sheathing,
almost clawlike. She wonders their taste

deepfried, as once in a younger life
she cooked mimosa blossoms, and still

does, cornmealed & black peppered,
the fruit, okra, Abelmoschus esculentus,

all those slime-succulent seeds, big
as fish eyes, as ideas, as soil

is reservoir, regulator, purifier, is
the stomach of plants. Well-hidden,

Kirsten & our kid, this hazy morning,
early, & they're watching the blossoms

unfold, exposed by it, seeing no movement,
and yet the flowers are a little more open

each time they look, as the dew is a bit
more gone back to air & the distance between

the rooster's bursts spreads, says
something about pace & process, how time

is change, anchorage, rootlet & runoff,
the coming frosts, continual humification,

the roaming. She's come looking for okra
to harvest – see the basket at her feet,

the one Sophie, oldest daughter, with guidance
from her Yaya, spiraled from materials

once tree. Pick the okra, snip pod at stem –
that's Ki's gig for now, which means handing

our boy William the stone he spotted &
then plucking some weeds adjacent, more

over there, geeking out over a caterpillar,
spiked, funky-hued pulser, &, O,

there are ripe red raspberries, the phone
is ringing, a truck tire on rumblestrip

over the low ridge – sound here does vista – over
the low ridge where a buzzard picks a tune

or two on a thermal. Now let's not get too
micromorphological or nothing – Woman,

she's picking okra, and buzzard's probably
hungry but having a good go of going

round. *Gracious*, Kirsten thinks, as Mr. Cheeks
taps now her side with stone-core fist,

good gracious, tomatillos taking over –
should have cut them back last fall

so as not to go to seed, volunteers. Got one
fine okra pod, nice length for eating,

she does – fingers on tip while with shears
in other hand she cuts & tosses it into basket

that buzzard might as well be weaving
a mighty tall though invisible

upper compartment for – the plant,
sprawly four footer, makes no show

of one pod being severed from it, as
if built to be picked, production

encouraged by it & so forth. *Ooh*,
boy on her back mouths. *Ooh, ooh,*

which means: I want that. Seems Mama
forgot her basket – she's wrapped

the length, green & ribbed & something
stickyhaired in her yellow nightgown,

a fold there – was a long night, not much
sleep as Waddlerboy's twin sister who

now stares at me somnambulating this tiller,
glares, really, from her place on a mulch on

cardboard path, not quite liking, no siree,
the noise or knowing without knowing how

tilling's not ideal, the way it chops worms,
burns gas, spreads weeds – best

the no till way where you add more goodness –
mulch, leaf, goat bedding – dung &

urine-soaked hay that's cooked down,
seedless. Ola's her name, after a woman

we've heard was some spunky & special –
Ola Lupton, my great great grandmother

who lived over the mountain around Bedford.
Ola Rose Moeckel, feisty & quick with it,

she's living up to lineage. Last night
she didn't much want to sleep, see, but roll

around, talk, make a ruckus, wake her brother,
all of us. Suppose the stalk, then, could be

the neck, roots the lungs & gullet both, among
other vital plumbing – it's that soil as stomach

of plants meme getting some fluff here,
expansion & stuff: the blossoms

the eyes, leaves the mouth, stems the ears,
fruit the nose. Funny mammal

at the end of this metaphor lane,
too funny but not worth passing up

a ride on. Mercy, my tunebox just shuffled
from Fine Young Cannibals' "Hard as It Is"

to Uncle Tupelo doing Little Feet's "Willin,"
and I like the aftershocks of the prior

seeping into the present song; and though
these earbuds really bite it compared

to tiller's Briggs & Stratton solo (ongoing
& digable), the riff's there & fine as that evening

by the woodstove when Ki & I were going
through seed catalogs, chose this okra

as much for its name as its description.
Edna Slaten's Candelabra: graceful,

branching plants, reaching shoulder height,
give great yields of 12 inch cowhorn-

type pods which remain tender even
after reaching a large size. The prickly pods

are a pretty, pale green...Originated
in Georgia. (20 seeds) $2.50. What pleasure

the writer of copy for seed catalogs must
know, though knowing in this case is not

necessarily to hold. I need to hold in
order to know a thing, need to work it,

too, for some years, at least, though even then
to know is more an admission of bafflement

and amazement so ripe it's best thrown
to the goats (be a goat, yo, you could

be one, harness the inner, and read this tilling
as a goat might, for the words but also

for the taste, the cud: chomp, chomparound?) –
and though Edna Slaten, whoever she is

or was, is in ways simply a name, it's that so
simply, a name fine for mouth & eye

just looking at it on the page that night
by Gracie the cookstove burning hot as

it had & would all winter, hot as carburetor
on tiller; sucking through, Gracie was,

that derecho-felled oak & cherry, a bit
of locust for coals through the night

into morning. I love how all the okra
in Baker Creek Heirloom Seed Catalog,

twenty two varieties, has a bit of lore
worked like flour into the description –

Bowling Red's been grown in the family
of that sporting name since *at least*

the 1920s. Burmese from – surprise! –
Burma. Eagle Pass from *around*

Carrizo Springs and Eagle Pass, Texas.
Emerald a Campbell's Soup variety

from 1950. Harlow's Homestead from
Tennessee. Also a Kentucky variety & several

from Louisiana, even a Filipino & one
Israeli one. Substance becoming &

rebecoming in a complex of clay & humus
under & in the four front tines – steel

boomerangs – doing their turning, their dumb
and beautiful, useful, damaging chain-driven circle;

turning fungi, the carpophores of certain polyphores,
while in compost, phyto sarcophagus, microphages

(nematode, springtails), gamasid mites; pedafauna
further down – woodlice, worms. Vertebrates

below that, & among, moles, shrews, other
critters our cats sometimes hasten their path

to soil for. Such moil, such swarm. Source,
& resource – so much grubbing for a way

to be. And do. Yesterday we were slicing okra –
couldn't write slicking – a good basketful

to lay in the dehydrator (easy way, no space
in freezer & such, for giving some gumbo flavor

to winter stews), and Kirsten said, *wonder
who carried the seeds, way back, from Africa*

over here. Hard telling, I said. *No heirlooms,*
she said, *from Africa in the catalogs.* I said,

None acknowledged. None, she said. Back
and forth behind tiller on hot, soft load

of life as immortal as it is alive, tenderly –
culture & time, people bearing the things

they know across oceans because it feels
right, just because, because here is pieces,

million pieces, & some you can carry. Vast
incorporation of organic substances – sex,

birth, growth, hope, hurt, love, & so on.
Dirt, it all comes down & rises to. Dig, dug,

let go of my eco – how do you add what
is added by it to be, the word is cooked, is

bathrobe, is torn Hefty of fleece from shearing
last with those French blades that turn

ampersands to dashes mongo or puny or
between. Need air spaces between particles,

though I do love clods, clumps, the way
surfacearth animates water, bears pressure of –

talking okra, talking marauder, choke lever.
See, twinsister Ola's eating peaches from that

compost volunteer now tree five springs
budded to. I hope she'll monge some maters,

cherry maters, too, from the sprawl we call
snack bar bed just east of herb spiral. I hope

she'll mind the bees among the, among
the squished & fermenting luscosities –

I mean peach & okra might marry in
a fraught though not unsavory way,

no? What do you sense? – and if it has
anything to do with what you know,

let's fork a bit of that mojo in bed's corner
for these tines to work into, and later the seeds

into flags, slender (& always cool to touch) flags
of arugula, *aahruerue*, let's call it, antithesis

of iceburg lettuce, mighty fine for pesto once
the basil's done bearing so much of what

pesto eaters say about the nut/oil/leaf/whatever
else (chevre, hogtongue, dried plum). Now

Kirsten's worked around the peninsula
of that okra bed, I think, because funny boy

and she are insight so fully out of it.
Earmulch, Tift Merritt coming now after

The Fiery Furnaces, Tift with her Carolina Triangle
high lonesome yum yum (gimme some),

and this machine is way out of harmony
except rollick the clamorlush hang on, the kid,

girltwin Ola, she alright? She alright, as if
there's any wrong. Much is wrong. There

are paths, there paths the bed, nettle bed,
walking onion, corn, peppers, maters,

beets, carrots, taters, interplantingnary travel
solward. Canopy of the under-atmosphere,

intimacies of, beyond of, & bonds. Till, brother,
till. Soil to be given back to once gifted must

in the cold dark cold quiet be amended
some more. Along the contour of the grade

for optimal water catchment & containment,
these beds do grow & service. Eight years back

this space yard parking for a mobile home,
and then chickens worked it, ducks (beak-

tillers), hogs, us, & these helpers we get via
a webnetwork, five hours a day willing vessels

to shovel, wheelbarrow, do whatever work
for room & board & help learning English

or just space, something different. About space,
I'm terrible, just jonesing for it, & of it,

in portions & textures that ooze of being &
of ease. And it's a gentle slope, shed on

one edge, rail fence rigor mortising to gate
to hurricane, that slatted wire weaving

seen turning beach & dune to a transition
where scarcity abounds squigglysmooth

as all get out – gentle with veggies, fruits,
herbs, worms, flowers, stalks, horizons,

the way the eyes with the tines go round,
up & down, as tillage edges in, five

and a half horse, the additives, relocations
of wood as ash, of manure as black gold,

of documents as shredded & coffeegrounded
in worm bin, of thought as sudden as hogsnooters

when they block the path of milk on its arc
from bucket to rubber tub, how the spray flecks

and shines, dotting oakboard, pantsleg, a freckle
or two on your cheek, curdled, cream-thick –

five gallons morning & night. Thank you,
Angie – hogs're happy you haven't started

that butterbidness. How they get down to it,
suck & slurp, stopping here & there to headbutt

as if such nourishment was meant to be private
or to say this is yummy, so good, we done

bumped our heads again. A fine day, William
and Ki in okra bed, Ola among peaches,

tiller & I having a walk, a real slow & sort
of strenuous back & forth little wrestle

of a walk. It's a mealtime, kind of;
I mean, smells so good – dirt, exhaust,

sweat starting to drip, glances to Sophie's beebox,
traffic there, to things needing moved,

fastened, rebuilt, torn down, recoated,
re-something or other. All about again,

making it do, doing it, home as making
(love, babies, dirt, okra, meal), dirt,

everything's dirt if not now then another
now, as in the goldfinch labyrinth, all those

sunflowers that've wilted from giving
so much to seed. Trances of haze baying

from hollow to ridge. Because glance
is sort of staring punctured, punctuated:

the green scalps of oak on Diamond Hill,
what's near what-ing what's wildest,

and Olu Dara in the ear: *Ella Mae, woman,*
come out your house now/I got some

fresh okra for you/Come get my okra,
okra,/come get my okra, okra. The word

is cornmeal, coated in. Okra, Bantu word:
ki ngombo or ochingombo. Now things turn

darker with the light, and maybe later
while the twins nap (let's hope they go

down easy today & for a while), maybe Ki & I,
we could take a bath in the rainbarrel back

of the barn & then hitch a team of crows, ride
west over the Alleghenies, sun in our eyes,

headwind keeping the pace casual, landing
now & then, but only for the ripest blueberries,

one or two, no more, to roll around the tongue,
the mouth, pasture being as much bed as land,

as something always has us in its scent here.
Sun, you old ridge runner. Sun, you softy you,

you shadowmachine. Dirt, too, is spent light,
and life rebecoming of that spent, spending. See,

there she is, the etymology of everything,
especially of seed. Like it, friend it, poke it –

the fact is facts blinker, and I'm liking this
sun, this heat, hands slick on tiller bar,

on cheap plastic grip from someplace far
& about as fathomable as underfoot & on,

the furtherunder. O life, this crazybrutal miracle,
and here comes Kirsten & boy, coming slow

to toddle hand in hand around chamomile,
chamomile, dagga, cabbage, peppers. Sun on hair,

her thickbrown. Nightgown reveal thing
going on being hunched like that down so

as to reach fat little hand & hold it, let it
hold. Shazam – I'm terrified I'm trying

to say, this dirt, I'm feeling brother
to it or closer, not even like it but it,

dirt – you are dirt, but that's okay, you,
dirt, that's okay, because it's good dirt,

soulful dirt, wormful. Earlier, old tooth
there was, mostly rust, off a sickle bar,

probably horsedrawn. That's not all,
never all – so many things, that's what dirt

is (not soil, be soiled even to speak it),
large numbers of little things, large being

quite, yes, quite a doggone understatement,
little, too, about how little or large who

can say. See that shadow there, it's not
but of me, of this stance in relation to tool,

chance but not chancy, bulking more
than moving, tremorish. Backfires,

the tiller – crisp boom – when I cut it. Twinboy,
in response, bloody murders. Tears, terror

primal as in no shred of knowing to it,
terror's vegetable mould – thanks Darwin,

Charles Darwin, Sir, late in life after The Origins
of it, the travels, now rooting & watching

and measuring the distance a stone in
his garden descends over 28 years

of wormwork, other wrigglers, & of
making calculations like Hendrix earlier

earbud-way, less calcing than ulating.
Ki asks me how's it going & I tell her

even though she knows more even through
her bare feet how. A *good harvest*, I ask,

and she confirms, says, *I'm leaving them.*
Leave them, please, I say. She does, so twins

and me, we eat some maters together, squish
juice, slurp them awhile before I say, *going*

back to tilling, kids, & they don't respond
but monge more maters, hardly pausing

when I fire up the engine, as I'm at distance
enough, less threat that way. The texture

of the place, poor model for egg carton,
but something like that, hills the teeth

of a grazer, deep time grazer. Turn, now,
tiller & I, and see the goats staring

this way, eager for some garden goodie
of a snack – nettles, comfrey, a few leaves

from a cornstalk. Peep them, the twins,
under the peach. Follow the tiller. William

sits, legs out, and works his hands through
the dirt. Ola's looking out to the west, up –

a buzzard there. Tiller I follow around now
we've come to end of bed. Back again

we go, this gasguzzling rooting hog
of a front tine picked up off Craigslist,

and whether it's riding me or other way,
hard telling. I like this machine, the work

of keeping it in line, in next place
that needs turned, hefting the heft of

the thing, finessing its wonky groove
and watching tines, mostly keeping legs

back, stance wide. Like sanding a board
from rough sawn to smooth, babybutt smooth –

monotonous, easy work, back work, back
and forth. As when a priming a thing for

its finish coats, there's time to reckon
the next stages, adjust the plan, ponder

the moves. We'll give this bed a couple
of days before setting the seed. Be, probably,

a salad mix, could be collards, beets, kale –
late season stuff. We'll let the storms

they're calling for, if they come, come,
and once this bed is dry, get the seed

in, get any chopped weed roots out
and gone, the wiregrass, the Johnson grass,

the this & that. Harder, really, this soft work
with its various mysteries, trust

and waiting, the weeding & watering &
watching for bugs. Give me boards

and concrete, hammer, nails, tape, shovel,
and I'll give you some poems long before

I'll give you a deck, no problema, o, a
might bit fussy here & there, but nothing

like what this tilling is easiest part of –
growing, dirtworking, seed & shoot tending,

surfing the soil, so to speak, riding the horizons,
what comes, & getting worked. Kirsten,

she's good at it, real good, a caregiver,
generous like that, a feel for things – rhythms,

the pulls & pools, shimmerings where human
and habitat commingle as insects do, like

she bears several senses beyond the usual five
or her five operate at a more sensitive bandwidth –

marriage like hers to place is, no joke, a form
of worship the way others betrothed to rivers & rains

that run in white between words as much as
in letterblack, and the difference between

looking and making is not the difference
between sleeping with your wife & sleeping

with your wife & your toddlers in a bed
too small, taking water over gunwales, those

daily devastations of cuteness (to quote
Mel Huber), being nightly too – O my, what is this

Diana Ross remix I'm swungulating both feet,
knees bent, in the air in some parody

of backscratch-manuva – tunebox sure
has my number today, playing out

the tiller mix – five senses, five vowels but
what about y – is that the sixth? I'll fuss

words & wood together in ways functional
enough, but in dirt work (& much other work),

I'm a little scattered, windblown, will always be
for reasons as – nothing new – psychometeorological

as physical. As in raising plants, so with children.
Now Kirsten's likely in the house going through

three boxes of toddler getup the Wilsons & Owens
handed down our way, (good duds, too – thanks

friends); while at the same time running water
for them & her for tea, & moving laundry

and chatting on the phone with Julie about
everything they chat about, including

but not limited to health, friends, work, kids,
family, food, each open to some way

to better tend to these life-parts. Suppose
the soil of marriage is children, and to say

you're married is to say you all have come
to till each other at times as only married people

with children & land & animals they work
hard for and love can till each other, not

flint & steel but acetalyne & puregrain,
but not brooms & vacuums, lists & bills,

not that either, no-sir-ee-bob-o-link,
we're talking the biochemistry of marriagedirt,

talking till in the voice of a cutie maybe three
years old who's just learned the word

from her big brother, along with some other,
let's say, choice words, and is walking –

this was long ago, Sophie a tike – walking
with your kid the same age also buck naked

in the yard, saying *till, till, till,* hissing it & giggling
and saying it some more or else saying

I'm going to tear off your head & till
down your neck. And the brain

of a plant is dirt, and a car's exhaust is more
dirt than the sound of its engine or distance

on odometer. I can feel it now, what the forecast
mentioned, those cells coming from Midwest –

could be here early afternoon. What time is it –
fourth or fifth diaper change o'clock?

Snack time thirty? Some doe goat must be in heat –
see that tail flipping around, who

is that, can't remember her name but now
Michelangelo's putting on mad airs through

the fence, red-slimy pencildick spraying
his face – what aim! Buck goats, all nuts.

That sound they make, origins of the word
tragic & bathos & holy moly in measures

not so equal, not so. Trathoshucks. Here comes
my good thing again & The Killers are doing

their anthem rock thing – fine tilling tune –
as she enters, garden gate-right, no longer

in her nightgown but a skirt & T-shirt
with Willie Nelson's mug on it, one

from the Five County Stadium show
in Zebulon, The Carolina Mudcats' home,

that perfect summer evening we sat in outfield
on a blanket, angels flying, as always,

so close to the ground; yes, she's fresh from
shower, hair up, face radiant, moist with oils,

a sort of over the shoulder stinkeye bearing
in my general direction, like I'm the buck

been wangulating all up in her sweet stuff –
yes, that's the woman who calls me,

among other things, husband, goofball, etc.,
and is mostly accurate, okay with that,

all for it, accuracy, love & fear the weather of
our twenty years, infiltrations each day,

seep of who's doing what when, all the static
and cling & what the luck. Nodule,

nodule & leghaemoglobin, grow
your okra while you can or fetch

a version from the store. I'm digging
this dirt, dirtdrunk, digging in circles

on this brainheart of the earth, neurons –
countless neurons firing, electric even

with nematodes. Plural of plural's end.
Worms & munchers & wrigglies puny,

punier, & less puny. The dirt is darker,
the nourished dirt that deserves so much

more than what we can give, the fear
and the love – which side (are there sides?)

are you on? – the dirt is not the silence. Dirt
appears silent. Crazyloud, the dirt, the aeration

and the thought of an infinite unthinking,
rearing dirt, rears. The dirt transforms, does

the nasty, more nasty. Is is is is is on top &
within more. The okra is dirt & dirt is is

and okra & woman & child picking there,
as well as man soiling them with his

intermittent stares, even his glances. Dirt,
butchered ramheads we buried last year under

where tiller now takes us, and how
when we dug them up eleven months after,

all was left was soft & scraggly remains as
of a sponge-scrubby combo run through

with the laundry to reuse too many times –
snack time soon, Kirsten tells me with so

many nonverbals as scrumptious as they
are clipped. I smirk & nod to kids – watch

your feet in these tines, man, pay mind –
and she follows, says with mouth & eyes

how peaches & tomatoes won't cut it, how
there'll be pesto with chevre to give it

extra goodstuff. My darlings, my relentless
darlings, they've toddled into the cornrows,

those teardrop beds arcing with the contour –
I hope you'll stay on the paths. You won't stay

on the paths. Low those paths are,
and what kid can resist an easy climb

on springy, soft, heavy smelling dirt,
especially when there are those cornroots,

rope coming to woven, strunting their stuff
from stalk's butt end, even a kind of stilting

going on with that basketry, like the roots
started too early, that leggy look. Tiller,

whack machine, its permajolt mode, arms
guiding it with least resistance possible,

a matter of haunches, torso, staying
with its tine-drive deeply gangly auto-

motion by keeping stance wide, some
dirt-turning grappler looking to avoid

being taken down. I want a hat, real tall
and pointed hat, felt or fleece, in likeness

of okra pod – I want to be its stem, to go
around in circles like that, to southeast

where twins in corn, the pasture sloping
to river, the cedars, fence, road, & so on –

counterclockwise down to south by east,
where the eye goes rarely, as ridge across hollow,

peaks, & longer, emptier ridges beyond are
more often (as if by horizon-gravity, some law

of looking around, optics, something), where
the seeing falls. Eyes have their habits, too –

here's the potato bed, dark dirt in mounds,
green & flaccid sprawl in eruption patient. Now

William, you're getting too close to barbed wire,
and your sister's going to follow you, O, what

can I distract, redirect you with? What combo,
fertile or not, what ionic swungdash of staring

at you & not having to turn off this machine,
break up the flow of turning dirt, carving

and grinding, sloughing & fluffing, sweet boy,
could work? A storm's brewing, kid! There goes

your sister now to join you, & why not? –
it's a fence, a border, and there's the promise

of goats, ewes, Pyrenees pups with Mama Stella. Food,
continuous food – what comes through eyes

comes through hands. I'm prepping a bed, slowly,
prepping a meal, not the next or even

close, & only part. Salad greens for this ground,
some kale, collards, Bok Choy as well.

There will be weeds. I like weeds. Weeds
are tough, persistent, do as much good, or

more, than any harm as long as they're plucked
before too darn long. Yum yum of bugluscious –

renew is the word. Beneath seeing getting it
on right now. Now & the news to come that

is – is it? – already here or has been, was.
Now's plural, dirt some Stretch Armstrong

of the soul of the now of the here of every
there being here & under, and we're not

adding value to this land, we're giving
our bodies & bodies to come a little care,

a little huenandaswirl. This ground, this
is where I'd like my enzymes to go

autocatalytic, my whole body to just go
to a metropolis of colonizing amazements –

illegal, you know, to bury your own on
your own ground, to eat your own's essence

that way. Kirsten's back in the okra now,
the kids sitting under the corn on dirt

on roots, some weeds & stones & crawlies,
squirmies, & so forth – they know. You know.

Once now I've been over this bed & twice
more the tiller & I & a couple gallons

of unleaded will go round & through – get it! See
Kirsten's moving last of last year's goat bedding

in wheelbarrow, spreading it on the beds,
and everything's so semi-woody, so about

to go to seed. Light is like that. And freedom,
scary bountiful – the work of home, the work of

what is dirt if not loyal, unswerving, hospitable
no matter what. I remember a day this past winter,

strange balmy, we were fixing up the raspberries
against where they meet the beds that Kirsten

now works old bedding in. There'd be snow
soon, a good couple days of it. Near the asparagus

we had a fire going, turning weeds to carbon smoothie
the snow would finish blending into soil, once

it melted. O, I'm not a gardener, don't get me wrong,
I'm a guy that likes being outside, eating well. The smell

of the smoke was the driplets of & under things.
Marital, I mean, sort of protofeverish. Totally waft,

premuddled. I mean only questions, the nature
of eating not always mouthmatter but as now

as then in winter to do with hands, calipers, shears,
a shovel, a mattock. Was a nice winter day, Sunday

I'm pretty sure since there were gunshots.
People around here like to shoot on Sundays.

Twins were doing their thing, helpless & trusting
as idiots, as angels, a little pinching, a little biting

and wailing among the brutal sweetnesses
of their play, warbles of noise only they understood

between them, calls & responses breaking
the sound barrier, so to speak. And I had

an ecstasy, I think, then, but I can't remember
what god, & couldn't then, or how the feeling

came or left, through what channels, orifices,
et cetera. And I didn't go inside to fix

a nice lunch. We'd eaten. I didn't stop invading
that Johnson grass where it had settled

and started to sprawl after coming in a load
of wood chips those dudes trimming trees

off local power line corridors gifted us.
We took ourselves off. Was a good day.

We were full for a while, even of emptying,
subnaked. Later a few friends stopped by. A day,

along with those before & to come, entwined.
Understand, I'm writing this poem with a tiller

in both hands. If you're with me at all,
you're getting the dirt & plenty of dust, too,

about being opened, broken, fantastically, to all
the shadows the ground will ever absorb,

I hope. Yes, this work is beyond the word.
We're reading, I hope, the sound of words turned

over at once from that which they were first
uttered, dirtmouth. Let the soil sound us,

if we can bear it, I'm tilling you, almost
wrote telling, this machine, how it lurches

when tine meets ledge, how I'm cored by the lathe
of no then. Holy, holy, holy. We can bear it.

And the despair of passion is dirt, & is, coffeegroundly,
of sensation, sheer, wondering the continuous,

as if a legacy of the underlands shaping the above.
Sound bites. *Dona got ramblin' mind,*

Dona got ramblin' mind, old time style,
Carolina Chocolate Drop style in tunebox

in pocket wired as if roots to earbuds
channeling it. Don't you stop tilling, boy,

heebie to the heebie & don't stop tilling, no
don't stop till naptime for babies now bawking

both of them over a rockshard one snatched
from the other. Snatcherama! The crow,

the buzzard. The sheep in the shade, goats
in the cedars. The sweat. The sweet. Will

there be a second haying? Will we get the house
of tentacles, the house of containment among

more pastoral modes or among the more
energy efficient. The twins – William cries now,

Ola stares as if considering how you see
crying before hearing it. What about those

collectors going postal over medical bills?
The repairs to hothouse? Last firewood? Fascia

on the new cabin porch for which I haven't
even primed the wood, though it's bought,

here, ready. Look, an oxidized thing – implement –
has been unearthed, a butter knife, & sucker's old

as the fork & spoon the tiller's gurgitated over
the years from beds adjacent. Cool now the kids,

playing fine, & I wonder who's getting Sophie
from her friend's house later. Will it be a drive

the twins to nap sort of trip? There, mockingbird.
There, bluebird. Moisture holding capability

and aeration increasing near feet I work to keep
to the side, compact less. Tines churn – they delve,

delve as they turn, grab, purchase, roll, roll.
Are rocks here – what's a garden without stone

to hold heat, moisture, give shape & structure,
memory of humping them from creek to truckbed

down the road in national forest, careful not
to pinch fingers or alert a ranger to such theft –

lugged some from roadcut, too, but most
are afterthoughts from evening swims

at the falls, nobody around but us so let's hump
a few rocks as big as we can handle to the truck

and then to garden where not only for structure,
generation of microclimates, habitats but as well

for mineral seep, another sort of mulch. My feet
are edgeways in path, not behind the tiller.

You know you can eat okra leaves. You can
extract oil from the seeds, a yummy cooking oil.

Amen to okra, to motherwort, copolymer penetrants,
chamomile, drive bolts that last. Steady, steady,

Pops, full throttle – get this bed all fluffed up.
Hurricane fence, chicken wire, locust post.

Rainbarrels, babies in their birthday suits now
chowing dirt as if mineral deficient. Here's

a worm, tine-chopped. Some grub. In
our marriagesoil – &, okay, you can tell

Kirsten I'm sharing this – I've mapped so far
nine horizons, and though this is far

from complete, there being upwards of
(data dump) 1.4 mil in the average partnership,

the dynamic interactions, or profile, of this
assembly of horizons might be worth

sharing – here (& remember it's all earth, water, light):
1/It started with a touch – there had to be a touch,

a wet finger. What it ended with was warmer
than the beginning, and less glittering. Glitter

had been dead a long time. Even the stuff
on cheeks & lips. Sometimes there was a leaf,

a cow bleating. Coming back was easy. You
were everywhere. Softer, in a way. The paulownia

shut its eyes. No, it blinked. And in the foreground,
where sound entered the picture like an abandoned

simile, there was fox musk. Consider this less
a postcard than notes made on the patch torn

from defiance's better eye. The creek had been
bankful, an oboe. Now it tambourined. 2/As though

there was motion beneath the internal, wholeness
even was scraped bark. Sure, trees need a good

rubdown. Sure, branchquiver held the plans in us,
grafted to the seven deadlies. Passing did not

mean without, we were told, and for years
rain invaded the easy, growing us, leaves

curled on those branches that are not like antlers
or like branches either. There was no end

to the leaves, anyway. We kept turning them
not over, but around – a soggy origami. Lord

knows they were wet enough, mold-soft, yet
erect in their way, certain nodes perky even.

Wilted were plenty of course. But wasn't plenty
the point. 3/So sun could burn through, making

shapes of – how long had it been? I don't mean
to gossip. I mean the past tense is often a metaphor

for significance. Look at one thing, like the shoal –
that's not one thing – how the curlers, little fingers,

type away; the sun on it that wasn't a minute ago.
It's minute, I know. We were scared. We could

have been living. Wouldn't that be funny. Yeah,
hilarious. Yeah, a gas. And the joy that was in

our sights, though we didn't know it, though
it was screaming, tugging us on leashes of

licorice. Calling us liars, calling us beautiful.
Please sing a bit. A rowdy song. Lightly. 4/

Splendor, you said, was disintegration, &
expansive, the way one thing was never one

thing. More a ricochet. More a multitude. A
be added. An etude. At least in those woods –

some double stuff in the downstream, the mountain
growing more brown. Deeper than hope could

stitch new cracks in lips, we inhaled. Like
each syllable was another species in the genus

of believing. Here came the wind. Here
came the leaving again. Not endings, we dwelt

on skulls, on the larvae of the lacewing. Passion
was tired of being heavy. Lacking chloroplasts,

glamour's lignum – we loved, loved by worlds
we couldn't name. 5/In silence we learned to speak.

In closeness we learned the anatomy of distance.
This woodpile, those stumps – by what hand & saw?

And for what fires? The pines upslope – it was
all root now, no, again. Everything coals. Briars

like paint on the light's canvas. In severity
we learned glee. What was afar lived again

and again & within. In pain we learned to smile.
Engulched, we learned wings. Wind, after wind.

Thermals of stone. It was all, and a striving
after seed. Not by accident, the echoes, but

openings. In study we learned to forget. In blaring,
to smart. But followings, pawprints. The dry clay

on the wet. 6/What version of flood had licked
the roots, we didn't know. But we lived by it,

immune to wind because the wind began
in marrow, everything else's. We ate what

we could. The woods were ticklered. And the fields,
too, seemed populated by vagrant blessings –

wrappers, worms – histories unaware of
their chronicling. All the trunks fingered the melt.

And you hung on in leaps, so ensphinctered
in unspeaking us from the very stone of light

becoming flesh. Consider a spiral – endolithic,
broomsedgey. Or a scribble. Probably science

had something to do with it. Or distance,
either. Truly, and breakage. 7/There, where

the green needles lay, where husk never ceased
its fall, that orb of beaks that said *bite me* –

we forked our pitched hearts, some roast rared
wonderfully, still a pulse. Call it moss-fodder,

the goal, a layer of humus less for laying
than bedding down. Sometimes there was trash –

truck springs, a can of timber marking paint.
Always the kermitude of ferns, wild ginger

like, like so many feeling words. I believe
the days played hangman with our breath.

What millennium was it anymore? I mean
the birds could give an eye so much, &

the days & the beholding, just by lighting
there, just by preening. 8/ Beginnings sure

had a way of fucking with us. But it was
so mammalian, so mammarian, the way the bark,

smooth for a stretch, came to a sphere of wrinkles
like yearning's relief map. We had to sit there,

we had to remember it even as we discovered it
growing as though a gift of forgiveness. Forget

the wreckage of the future we were living in.
I think we had given up hope of a better past

and were kids again, citizens of a wiser age,
whenever that was, following the footprints

of mist. Likewise, the water ran a wider course,
some Sistine of stick & stalk, silt gathering,

rising against the depth. 9/Again we witnessed
the days teaching woe how to laugh, smooching it

till it giggled. We almost missed walking out
so dead to ourselves that a piece of shit was

plenty of amazement. It was different then,
the people told us, and normal not to trust them.

The images were the same, the settings the same
and probably the motives, too – to woo life

astonishing, to see the shrubs shine, to praise
and jibe. To dance on the roof of love's outbuilding.

Yes, to kick & sway along that pitch, seeing a piece
of shit as a piece of shit, the sun as the sun, the moon

as the sun, and the heavens of difference in both
of them. That's that. Clods earlier, now ellipses. I know

nothing of the heart of what plants or what
if everything is just nutrient uptake as in Kirsten

in the okra fetching for another round of
getting some ready for winter. I've got a grip

but the grip's not mine – it's tiller defined,
it's days, endless, playing after gradeschool in

the mudball factory in the woods behind
the house. Dirt, clay, soil, humus, mould.

Plantstomach, rooting zones. Intestinal,
infinitesimal secretions. The color of the dirt,

the color of badass farm chick shifting gears from
okra harvesting to plucking wiregrass, other

weeds too, from among the peppers. In headsoil
I could hand-dig a pond, a little a day a time, see

if we can get it right, place it as if by some
dowser's fortune & feeling where water's likely

to rise. Meanwhile the dogs often go bonkers
after a sirensound coming over the ridge. Sun

in vision smudgy & in rest of body's gathering
of such information, the totality between wearing

insulated muck boots with shorts & the way
the cicadas, millions of them, this being

the seventeenth year, left holes from bottom
up most everyplace in lawn, pasture, beds

earlier this summer. They are gone now mostly
to share that dirt with larvae of offspring in,

say it – soil is as much incest as the soul of
a place once it's worked out of being space

and the hairband of space, the one in the rocks
once you cross bridge at trailhead where this

is dwelling forks off right away & we usually
stay tuned to various forecasts for high humidity

afternoons along the seam of space becoming
place because you work it, think on it, feel it

every single way you can, even how the dirt
is alphabet the plants are speech of, some shit,

the various spellings. Capillary action. Sam Cooke,
Sigur Ros (not good tilling music), Parquet Courts,

Flat Duo Jets (fine tilling music), Galaxie 500,
No Strings Attached, Madder Rose, Dwight

Yoakum, Brady's Leap, DJ Spooky – tunebox
churning it out on random under some

Briggs & Stratton heavy background drone,
and it's all – or is it? – coming through hands

into tiller's grip & down through tiller into
the dirt, a subsonic vibration, magnetic maybe,

stirring worms & other, more teensy grubbers
there, not the way the music on jambox lives

on in house where it was played while being
built – you hear it best just after snow has finished

falling at night, & the moon's big, & you're trying
to sleep but you want to be kicking & gliding

on skinnies around & across the pasture
but your head has turned bowling ball under

a cold. Relentless, raising twins, relentless
the fretjoytediumwonderpouringpleasure –

I'm loving this, you see, this tilling, this
brainless turning & following with tunes

in ear & cumulonimbus shapeshifting there &
above as Kirsten does now on knees adjacent

comfrey & cardoon, fetching a few red raspberries
for pick-me-up, fruit of the labor & whatnot –

a break, this tilling is, break from swarm of, of
mist kids require though mist it's a kind of,

of care that hardliner contingent do frown upon –
look, well-intentioned nincompoops of no till school,

we've added plenty, will add more to this bed:
more sawdust, ash, leaves, manure, bone, urine,

straw, grassclipping, eggshells, oystershells,
coffee grounds, old socks, shredded paper,

dunnage fleece & so on – you name it, we might
add it, even your voice, your internet provider,

most longed-for name. Goldfinch, contrail – as
warning label is to biomass, ugly word,

there're acres of polyculture here, & under them,
under only one, the equivalent of ten draft horses

in critterenergy, or so I've heard. For now
the story: tillerforce & harnessing it so

no perennials or other good rooteds get torn up
should I lose step in this dronedance some

might call control, what work is, force,
counterforce so as to direct original

in service of an end one hopes the process of
is meaningful for belly, at least, if not

eye, heart, knuckle, soul, the whole shebang.
To till is to type a letter to God in the dirt,

a nice note that says thank you, help me,
this is a good thing, a beautiful, lucky thing

to be able to do with my wife & kids on
a fine day, & bless us, let us trust your will

for us, this dirt, whether or not it serve as
we hope & aim-wife it so. No, or maybe –

to till is to take a walk, a recirculating, hey,
semi-rectangular & shifty sort of walk,

meaning giving ground some heavy duty
inacupressure with steel fingers not really

extensions of your own. What could save
could bring us closer to the essence

of wonder & horror, all the academies
bleary-eyed & who the hell else knows

what all else – I mean, is everything in life
not dirtwork more fear & hiding? – crapstorm

of media, opinions, banter, ballyhoo, art,
money, politics, fast cars, the old in/out

yearning & naught – so much barking,
humdingering & so tasty, these bedevilments.

A Swiss chard, this corner, & there a sunflower,
and each time we cut it close, tiller & I,

pebbles rise as other matter courses down,
sidelong & down, in the fluid medium, a living

and thickchanging flow, water in waves, in
slow waves that hold & grow us as we are

and so much more, it's load. And what if
there's one common substance & all of us

are merely forms, matter consistent, a force
manifest, remanifesting in flux continual –

*have you ever seen a she gator protect
her young,* Skynard croons from tunebox

in that song once cracked me up but not now
not with this half-mantis, half-bulk of

an oil-churning MTD tiller turning body
and brain to a scramble, a congeries

of horizonjolts. I love this world, love
the messes & miracles in the messes,

the way things come in & heat up & settle
into changes, life's strafings. Of course,

it'd be fine to forage our food, not have
to mess with all this but fetch it from

the wild as if there's enough in or of
the wild. Maybe love's life is love's afterlife,

but this, this is cultivated foraging,
still a gift, what soil gives, is, all

its has beens becoming this continual
unbecoming into a post-forest forest

pure shadow, source & end continual,
all of this way back only woods, &

wayer back, seas, plates colliding
and then coming apart. A blind life

down there, here, now time-altered –
or not, who knows what nematodes

know, if it's like one big snowfall
all the time, & always more, that hush

and density, that probing of the melt &
the hardening up, with refreeze, as in

drier times, day & night not photogenerated
but a matter of action, scents & sense

a more spritely if not vigorous noodling,
the way our little home has changed

since the relentless cuteness & need,
the wonder & fatigue these dirt munchers,

these fragile & amazing munchkins
that are our second & third munchkins –

they mulch us, these kids, as the older one,
Sophie. They make us better & worse

at the same time. We fester. We burn,
love's squirmies, duty's exhaust – the heart

breaking down to host, to open & nourish.
Do you wriggle at this? Where's the irony?

I hope you're wriggling. I'm wriggling –
see, this isn't man versus nature, not man

versus God but versus part that says
this isn't miraculous, that says who are you

and why are you doing this & with whom
and how did you get here, why have you

been so lucky to stay & who the hell
would ever listen to any of this, Lord

knows – it's a surrender, that's the ticket
to this small labor on this small patch

of ground with machine fetched one
spring day off a dude, sad, resigned guy,

lived off Hershberger, had to mention
the divorce, make the sale sort of guilttrippy

and weird. Here's how we do it, did this, & you
can too, those are the verses, these, how to

fail & fail & fail & fail & fail & fail
the only story worth telling as long as day

is made clear in all its panopterial splendiferocity
of the zoink, some iron in the dirt riffing

on home & how home gets all up under your heel
in your boot where it plips over cuff – neoprene –

of the muck. Word is dirt, & action is dirt,
and worm is action as deeper into this tilling

I go the more each letter becoming rootlet
absorbs, anchors, secretes. Words blur,

they stain – and they foster to the nil
of the ninety first savoring the sound barrier

of time & seeing, & I'm no farmer, you know,
I'm a podcast, I'm a dirty podcast,

sexy Mama's troublesome farmhand trying
to get some tilling done before the storm, before

twins need to nap & need stories, a few of them,
read/invented with a lullabyplane carving

voice's thermals, lilty & customized to occasion,
details from the body, the present eternity

that obliterates now into fruiting bodies
that pierce, I tell you, prick & pierce in

an augury of new translations from
the protozoan. You know the gig. The body.

The sky, the jolting. The meanwhile & how the clouds
are not some laundry but some spin cycle,

and as for me I can't forgive my appetite
for all this avoiding the word luminous

such that not even being is. Or is more.
That line, the fourth up from here, some

could be, with a little rain, soma, so let it
after the tilling's done, seeds in, &

let us let the rain be on our faces even
when I'm singing for the umpteenth

Raffi's "Wheels on the Bus," "Baby Beluga,"
"Brown Bear, Brown Bear, What Do You See" –

I see two toddlers in the mint bed & black widows
in the mint bed too, & that's a problem

even if the latter's a mind eye trace
of memory kind of seeing. Love always feels

closest when I can't read my own handwriting.
What about you? Do your buzzards prefer

clockwise? Have you invented happenings
such as the festival of cicada pot pie

to be held every seventeen years, those Junes
you can't hear yourself think or even

listening, pulsations of whirring are
so much? Did you stop talking to your mother? –

if so, for how long & what was the result?
Did you spank your child for just being

a child? What pair of socks do you like most
to wear on cold days? Have you sensed a w/hole

in the universe every time somebody spoke,
and did you call it love? How long since

you saw your sister or sent her a card?
Have you written a letter on the back

of a label peeled from a can of something
you hope to never again have to eat. One day,

by the grace of some deity, you'll say
the word wet & actually feel it – I hope

it's soon, that fine day. This is not a transcription
of what the dirt says under the tires, let's

be clear at least about that distraction
and whatever other sweatstains be they

on your worn to soft perfection sweatshop-built
boxer briefs or those affecting your vision. Dirt,

and in my pocket a knife. In the air a heat
and a resistance, a balm that is a resistance

of thunder & light, not far. Slide the lever to *off*.
Stand back, let the backfire be a cough,

a sigh. Let your ears adjust & see the way her fingers do,
Kirsten's, with clarity & rhythm – are they dissimilar? –

as in kitchen now, she chops, chop, eight, ten times
per okra pod, the pause between, & again,

to slice another batch, little wheels, some
wobbling a bit, most on side – no, it wasn't okra

but some cut trunk with growthrings so concentric
it might have sparked the thought, hey,

this would roll with another attached by
a fastener, as in axe & axle might have more

in common than any than. Edge-ways,
her knifeblade to form okra chips,

the bumpy wheels, into a mass the more easy
to slide on the fine screen, stretched, of

the dehydrator trays, & even now, cutting
like this, I see her move across the garden

as if it was her mind, not thinking but plucking
okra, weed-snatching, & kid-wearing, watching out

for all of it, the good & the less good than what good
might mean in your lines, lines of ryegrass, lines

of leaning in & paying mind lines & empty
mind care lines so as to know what the what

never says but means by circling it, chowing down
under the center where paying attention

isn't reborn but sure as shit could be again
and again. The okra is body. The body

of a tangled body, a pre-postmystical body –
I mean she moves among the crops as an insect

with body & wing slight enough to make
the wind its primary navigator. And that – hers –

is some wind, like she is & isn't blowing it &
being blown by it herself, from some external

yet to be known self, letting itself be known.
She moves like spring – we're as far from spring

as spring, even near, is far – it's like everything
green in her is another sun, like talent for her means

being at home – being home giving to ground
because ground is part of her body as though

the children of her body, the makers & unmakers
of her body, & the bodies of water that bear

her body's effluent now, as well as all those
that have in the past, in prior or visited habitats.

Last night I stood in quarter moonshadow growing
each night less gray with the waxing. I said, Dirt,

we could be on the river now. It's bright enough
even now, full moon still three days off. Dirt

just sat there – maybe it heard me. I admit a heaviness
in both ears, a thickness, there being North Creek water

in both after a brief evening swim, a good
waterfall backrub spot, deep pool for

a few strokes & glide. Dirt, I continued, do you
ever dream of a government that asks first,

before any decision is even considered, how will this
affect the dirt? – because it believes (a given)

that dirt is soul of citizenship, that being
all beings, that citizenship – and then because it

(government) has decided (without even having
to decide), therefore knows that how we raise

our food, gather other energy – heat, cooling,
transport – does, in part, determine the quality

of our energy, ourselves & communities – but
I lost dirt here & there was a shooting star, the fences

suddenly creepy & great. I mean, there's no more
tilling sound. The tunebox quiet too, twins

playing all hushed in the gravel drive. Knife
through okra on cutting board. Another, another,

and this tiller done turning dirt's wrists
to mush. Dogs bark. More thunder. I leave the beds,

dunk under rainbarrel's brass mouth. Hands, head,
neck. This, too, is dirt, as my friend, Rob, father

of my daughter's two bestest – they left last week,
moved to Maine, Rob, his wife Judy, all the kids

and stuff, gone for religious reasons. Rob
could see tree in terms of board feet, worked

as a forester, & yet he saw them at once, & more
deeply, as holy. Rob was dirt, okra, made music

with a chainsaw, terrible & fluent movements –
those trees passed on with staggering grace. Not

a big guy, Rob. Was ropey, straight up, a
bit bent, but it was uncomplicated,

our friendship. I met him through Kirsten, who
met Judy and kids at the farmers market

in Lexington, where they both womanned tables,
peddling good eats in the parking lot behind the place

that serves a chocolate pecan pie with – get this –
homemade marshmallows. Gonna miss Rob, his family,

gotta send them some dried okra up to Maine, see,
the dirt's good now, porous, well sorted, fine,

and there's a storm nearly here, coming over
Purgatory Mt. just now, and one morning

last week, as I hauled water to chickens,
fetched eggs, there was the sound of this storm –

I know that now – the sky clear, not even the body odor
of a cloud. Your guess is as good as freezing rain

getting a second chance to find the ground
as temperature rises above what water needs

to think its way out of being a solid. O, dirt, say
troublesome is too generous. Say blathering

more like it, say blathering with in your ears
and on most of your body save where sweat

streaks it, some Zamboni of flesh where
exertion's the rink, being's zinc. I mean,

here comes Ola, William on her tail.
They're lighter. No more combustion. They

also want to play – is it wash? splash? be? –
in the rainbarrel. I'm going to hold them first,

squish Ola now, she's here, then her bro.
You never know what tilling will perform.

Acknowledgements

Grateful acknowledgement is made to David Young, Jonathan Farmer, John Hoppenthaler, and the others who work at *Field*, *At Length*, and *Connotation Press*, where parts of these poems were first published.

I would also like to thank Aaron Baker, Philip Brady, Suzi Branch, Gerald Breedon, Tommy Eubank, Jon Guy Owens, Morgan Wilson, The Whitt Family, The Nelson Family, The Preece Family, The Lenoir Family, Brent Zimmerman and Valerio at Valle di Mezzo, and my neighbors, students, and colleagues, without whose assistance and encouragement this book would never have been completed.

Further thanks are due to The National Endowment for the Arts, Hollins University, and The Jackson Center for Creative Writing.

Endless gratitude to my family – and to the flocks, herds, and beds: *wild tending.*

Books from Etruscan Press

Etruscan Press Is Proud of Support Received From

Wilkes University

Youngstown State University

The Ohio Arts Council

The Stephen & Jeryl Oristaglio Foundation

The Nathalie & James Andrews Foundation

The National Endowment for the Arts

The Ruth H. Beecher Foundation

The Bates-Manzano Fund

The New Mexico Community Foundation

Drs. Barbara Brothers & Gratia Murphy Endowment

The Rayen Foundation

The Pella Foundation

Founded in 2001 with a generous grant from the Oristaglio
Foundation, Etruscan Press is a nonprofit cooperative of poets and
writers working to produce and promote books that nurture the
dialogue among genres, achieve a distinctive voice, and reshape the
literary and cultural histories of which we are a part.

etruscan press
www.etruscanpress.org

Etruscan Press books may be ordered from

Consortium Book Sales and Distribution
800.283.3572
www.cbsd.com

Small Press Distribution
800.869.7553
www.spdbooks.org

Etruscan Press is a 501(c)(3) nonprofit organization.
Contributions to Etruscan Press are tax deductible
as allowed under applicable law.
For more information, a prospectus,
or to order one of our titles,
contact us at books@etruscanpress.org.